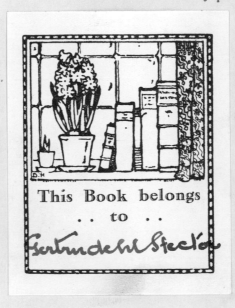

This Book belongs
.. to ..

Gertrude M Hector

# LITERATURE IN MY TIME

# LITERATURE
## IN MY TIME

*by*

### COMPTON MACKENZIE

LONDON
**RICH & COWAN LTD.**
Maiden Lane, Strand
1933

*First published October,* 1933

PRINTED AND BOUND IN GREAT BRITAIN BY R. CLAY & SONS, LIMITED,
BUNGAY, SUFFOLK, FOR MESSRS. RICH & COWAN, LIMITED,
27 MAIDEN LANE, LONDON, W.C.2

*My Dear Francis:*

*I have inscribed this book to you to commemorate above all our friendship; but in choosing your name on this occasion I have been influenced by an anxiety to insist upon the personal aspect of* Literature in My Time. *If I have seemed to avoid any attempt to estimate the work of most of my immediate contemporaries in the same field of literature, it has been entirely due to a distrust of the fairness of my own opinion. I have taken advantage of the title to indulge the egoism of the impressionistic critic, and I have mentioned no book which I have not read myself. You will know that what may seem provocative is merely the expression of an opinion so firmly held that honesty forbids its exclusion.*

*Yours ever,*

COMPTON MACKENZIE

*Ardveenish,*
 *Island of Barra,*
  *July 31, 1933.*

v

# CONTENTS

# CHAPTER I

THE reading of childhood is for most of us the great opportunity of our lives to ignore what is strictly contemporary in literature. That reading resolves itself into three classes. First there are the books written expressly for the entertainment or instruction of young people. Secondly there are the books written for adults but considered suitable for young people and recommended to them by their seniors. Lastly there are the books which young people find out for themselves, the discovery of which so often leads to censorship and prohibition. My own reading, from a variety of circumstances, was never interfered with during the first eight years of my life, and I missed the experience of having *Jane Eyre* snatched out of my hands and locked away in an inaccessible cupboard. I mention *Jane Eyre* particularly because it is the book of which most people now in their fifties will remember having been deprived. Actually *Jane Eyre* was not in my father's library, and thus a kindly fortune spared me the disastrous emotional experience of reading *Jane Eyre* in immaturity, for I would accuse Charlotte Brontë of having inspired more bad novels and cultivated more bad taste in reading than any other writer of genius. The Victorian woman who thought that Miss Brontë had cheapened her own sex was justified in such a belief. The sight of a woman lying on her back and kicking her legs in the air is not pleasant. That was what Miss Brontë seemed to her contemporaries to be doing, and we may guess that her sneers at the novels of Miss Austen were due to the conviction she must have had that the older and greater writer would have recognized what she was doing and disapproved of such a lack of self-control. Even now *Jane Eyre* should not be read under thirty.

# CHAPTER II

*Alice's Adventures in Wonderland* published in 1865 and *Through the Looking-glass* published in 1871 still seemed intensely modern in the 'eighties. The juggling with the English language fascinated children, for the appeal to the primitive of a play on words is universal, and Lewis Carroll may be credited with a profoundly disturbing influence upon the formation of a youthful mind during the last quarter of the nineteenth century. The significance of Lewis Carroll was that his fancy had illuminated the possibilities of ordinary existence, particularly in *Through the Looking-glass*. Few rooms in the 'eighties were without a mirror over the mantel-piece, and it was a bold child who felt perfectly convinced that, could he like Alice find himself in that contrariwise world, he should be able to deny its reality. He was ready to admit the improbability of reaching that world; but he could not deny the possibility of its existence in the present, whereas whatever his faith in fairy stories like the collection of the brothers Grimm they could only be true once upon a time. It would hardly be too much to claim that Lewis Carroll prepared the mind of the average man to accept the truth of relativity, the stellar arithmetic of Sir James Jeans, and the swirling

phantasmagoria of psycho-analysis. The tales
of Hans Andersen that affected myself and my
childish contemporaries most deeply were those
like *The Ugly Duckling*, *The Tin Soldier*, and
*Big Claus and Little Claus*, in which the
ordinary objects of humdrum life were trans-
muted into an extraordinary reality. That life
beneath the river discovered by Little Claus
possessed the same kind of disturbing possibility of truth as that life through the looking-
glass.

The appeal of *Struwelpeter* to the childish
mind, which persists to this day, is not easy to
perceive. Presumably when the book was first
published it was intended to exert a serious
moral influence, and even in the 'eighties,
although the bright crude pictures illustrated a
manner of life foreign in place and remote in
time, they possessed a recognizable actuality,
perhaps because the bad behaviour of the various
children could still be linked with our own bad
behaviour. Our sisters were not dressed in
pantalettes like Harriet, but they did sometimes
play with matches; and the carmine-topped
vestas which in those days were a common
feature of the smoking-room had at least some
of the dangerous qualities of the great lucifers
with which Harriet played, and by which she
was reduced to a small heap of smoking ashes.
Some of us, like Conrad, still bit our nails, and

the sudden entrance of the long-legged Scissor Man was still an unpleasant possibility. Like Cruel Frederick we were inclined to persecute flies, and there were still emotional moments in the nurseries when we reduced our Marys to tears. We still fidgeted at table like Philip. Like Augustus we found certain dishes uneatable, and we still had fits of absent-minded progress like Johnnie Head-in-Air. To be sure, Robert's ascent into the sky at the end of an umbrella was beyond our credulity, and the growth of humanitarianism had made the behaviour of Edward and his companions in mocking the Blackamoor seem an improbable exhibition of bad manners for ourselves; but in the last quarter of the nineteenth century most children were still under the influence of the old Puritan idea that the Creator was subject to abrupt fits of explosive wrath, in the course of which he was apt so far to abuse his omnipotence as to strike some wretched child blind for reading a secular book on Sunday afternoon. *Shock-headed Peter* was a *reductio ad absurdum* of the three centuries of Puritan domination over the manners of Great Britain, against which, like all children throughout that domination, we rebelled, but of which we were still afraid.

Moreover, we were still reading books like *Holiday House* in which, notwithstanding the rigours of Mrs. Crabtree and her tawse, Miss

Sinclair's young hero and heroine performed feats of naughtiness that left us gasping. Whence arose the contemporary notion that children during the nineteenth century existed in a condition of depressed virtue? A perusal of early nineteenth-century juvenile literature reveals an active wickedness which makes the indulged child of to-day a poor anæmic little creature in comparison. I remember reading at the same time *Sandford and Merton* alternately with a volume of the *Newgate Calendar*. Presumably the wicked Merton's ability to hold his own with highwaymen and murderers was the attraction.

Of books of adventure those which stand out in my memory with particular vividness are *Robinson Crusoe*, *Coral Island*, and *The Swiss Family Robinson*. Fenimore Cooper, of whose enchantment of the youthful imagination I still hear, was never read by myself or my friends. We attempted *The Deerslayer* and *The Last of the Mohicans*, but found them dry, that damning epithet of youth. The tales of Captain Marryat, except for *The Children of the New Forest*, were ceasing to play a vital part in the entertainment of the youthful mind. We preferred W. H. G. Kingston as a nautical writer, and presently his sea-stories were to be displaced by such productions as *The Iron Pirate* of Max Pemberton. It is worth noting that with the development of machinery the quality of juvenile literature deteriorated. Jules Verne got the best out of it in anticipation. In the end machinery may kill all art.

Of school stories the one which is always derided as typical of the kind of school story to which youth at the latter part of the nineteenth century was chained is *Eric, or Little by Little*. My own recollection is that none of us read it. On the other hand, we did read Dean Farrar's other story, *St. Winifred's, or The World of School*, and we derived from it the keenest pleasure. Physical bullying was still prevalent in the 'eighties and early 'nineties, and, though none of us was likely to be let down out of dormitory windows at night in order to smuggle in spirits for the delectation of senior boys, we could most of us include in our experiences of life the misery of subjection to tyrants. However, the school stories we really enjoyed were those of Talbot Baines Reed. The excitement of the serial appearance of *The Cock-House at Fellsgarth* in the *Boys' Own Paper* of 1891 is still warm in my memory and only matched in that same year by the serial appearance of the *Adventures of Sherlock Holmes* in the *Strand Magazine*. *Tom Brown's Schooldays*, except for a few isolated incidents like the adventure with the gamekeeper and the School House match, was voted both pi. and dry. Several crusades to

make me read the book were launched, but even
the possession of a copy inscribed to me by
Thomas Hughes himself in the year 1886 would
not persuade me to read it through. *Tom
Brown's Schooldays* is described thus in that
excellent compendium by Dr. Ernest Baker,
*A Guide to the Best Fiction in English*: " . . . the
love of truth and manliness, Tom's honesty,
loyalty, and reverence for what is better than
himself, make, and were intended to make, a
strong appeal to young readers." I wonder.
Speaking for myself, and I do not think I was
exceptional, I used to excise sentences, pages,
nay whole chapters on account of their kinship
with the "pi. jaw." For us the figure of the
Doctor was already as much a figure of fun as
one day Lytton Strachey was to make him in
*Eminent Victorians*.

The part that Doctor Arnold played in the
creation of the English public-school tradition
has been exaggerated. What to some seems an
elaborate structure of humbug, to others an
admirable system of practical stoicism, to others
again an ideal application of the taboos of
primitive peoples to civilized education, has
always been inherent in the English character,
and it was as evident in the public-schools of the
eighteenth century as it is to-day. If cribbing
was disgraceful it was only disgraceful in the
same way that sheep-stealing was disgraceful,

as an attack upon property. Morality did not enter into the matter. If bullying decayed, the decay was due either to a loss of vitality, or more probably to a diffusion of vitality in a world of rapidly widening opportunity. The English public-school exists to provide an Englishman with an assurance of class superiority. By virtue of that class superiority he despises not merely those not of his class but the whole of the rest of the world, or rather he did despise them until recently; but with the shaking of his belief in the infallibility of the public-school system his belief in the superior destiny of the English race has been shaken at the same time. Hence many of the problems of the present that assail him.

On reading again *Tom Brown's Schooldays* in maturity, some of us can discern the immortal essence of boyhood which was hidden from us when we read it first as boys; but the perfume is growing faint and cannot last much longer. To those who have grown up after a post-war education it can say nothing. To them it must be more of a curiosity than a book like *The Fairchild Family* was to us, for if the psychological approach to the schoolboy has not changed, the externals have changed so profoundly that even a school story which made a wide appeal in the last decade of the nineteenth century can have no hope of survival. In *The*

B

*Cock-House at Fellsgarth* the drama was provided by the rivalry between the classical side and the modern side, and in those days as a matter of course the angels were all on the classical side. The "moderns" were inferior beings. I well recall the compassion I had for those who were on the modern side of my own school. That secure superiority has vanished now. When the University of Oxford betrayed culture by abolishing compulsory Greek for Responsions the way was clear for the Americanization of the English public-school. In the future a genuine education on modern lines may be evolved, and this painful period of transition become merely an unpleasant memory. Yet the example of America does not encourage optimism. Nor does the Arts course of any Scottish University.

There were many other books of our youth I should like to mention, but the danger of sentimental glorification is always imminent, and it is wiser to cut the list short. There is one author, however, whose influence is so beneficial that I cannot refrain from taking an opportunity to urge her presence in every house where there are young people, and that is Juliana Horatia Ewing. *Melchior's Dream* is certainly one of the greatest short stories in the English language, and its appeal to the imagination of childhood is infallible. Stories like *Our Field* and *The Great*

*Emergency* and *A Bit of Green* offer a magical introduction to human nature, and their absence from the average nursery and schoolroom of to-day is a serious loss. Their limpid English, their sentiment which never degenerates into sentimentality, their revelation of the human heart, and their moral lessons so exquisitely concealed are beyond my poor attempts at praise. Perhaps more copies of *Jackanapes* and *Daddy Darwin's Dovecot* and *A Flat Iron for a Farthing* exist nowadays on nursery shelves than I have been fortunate enough to find. But I fear I am right in thinking they are gone.

It is a delicate matter to criticize the children's classics which have appeared since I was a child myself, but except for *The Golden Age* and *Dream Days* of Kenneth Grahame (and these are really children's books for grown-ups) I cannot surrender to any of them. All seem to me tainted with the avuncular self-consciousness of *Peter Pan*. "Once upon a time" has become the Children's Hour of the B.B.C. Those synthetic monsters, the Teddy Bear, the Golliwog, and the Kewpie, have established themselves, and their mythology is already extensive. Christopher Robin goes jiggety-jig, and his jiggety-jiggery suits the age. To A. A. Milne belongs the honour of enshrining with urban romance the civilized and comfortable child of to-day. *When we were Very Young* marks an epoch as positively as any children's book has ever marked one. It is not extravagant to surmise that a distant posterity may find in that volume of children's verse a key with which to unlock the present more easily than with any contemporary novel, or poem, or play.

# CHAPTER III

## SOME OF THE BOOKS WE WERE TOLD TO READ

WE may presume that there has been no period in which grown-up people have recommended to children the novels of contemporary renown. Thackeray was not considered a suitable novelist for our grandfathers to recommend to our fathers, just as Hardy was not considered a suitable novelist for our fathers to recommend to us. Yet by some strange freak of the parental mind there is no hesitation in supposing that the novels which appealed to them in their prime will appeal to their children in their nonage. Thus, as a matter of course, *Pendennis* and *Vanity Fair* were put forward in my youth as good books for twelve-year-olds. Possibly in this parental habit may be found an explanation of the way each successive generation of youth seems to enter life in a state equipped to deal with progress, and why parents are heard expressing bewilderment at the advanced ideas of that younger generation. A book like *Vanity Fair* formerly struck hardened men of the world as cynical, as cruelly cynical, as dangerously cynical. Yet we were invited to read *Vanity Fair* at an age when cynicism should have been a great deal more dangerous than it ever was to the hardened men of the world who read that great novel when it first appeared. What I find significant is that such books of Thackeray or Dickens as I read in my nonage I can again with pleasure now when a good deal of the world is behind me, and that those of their books I did not happen to read then I find it impossible to read now. It is easy to believe that I did genuinely appreciate *Pickwick Papers*, *Dombey and Son*, and *David Copperfield* when I was a boy; but I confess I find it very difficult to belive that I appreciated *Vanity Fair*. Yet I must have derived from it the illusion of enjoying a vital experience, for otherwise I should not be able to make that early reading of *Vanity Fair* a permanent foundation for reading it again.

Not that these light-hearted recommendations of classical novels by our elders were always successful. Jane Austen was early pressed upon my attention, but I was well into my twenties before I was able to enjoy the work of one whose work I now enjoy above that of all other novelists.

The real battle in my youth was over Scott, and the brutal truth that by the last decade of the nineteenth century we had outlived Scott must be coldly set down. The blame for this is usually placed upon the ill-advised forcing of him upon children as a holiday task. The cause lies much deeper than that, and it is noteworthy that we were only able to enjoy his second-rate novels like *Ivanhoe*. *Guy Mannering*, *Old Mortality*, and *Redgauntlet* bored us. So far as he was an influence on our youthful reading it was an influence like Lytton's. I hate to call it tinsel romance, feeling in myself a kind of treachery in so doing. Yet who would hesitate to call *The Last of the Barons* or *Paul Clifford* tinsel romance? And with them must be classed, in spite of all the protests of our natural piety, *Ivanhoe*, *Kenilworth*, and even *Quentin Durward*. Now, if ever any boy should have been naturally disposed to enjoy Scott at his best it was myself. I knew almost by heart his *Tales of a Grandfather*. His Jacobitism, timid though it was, refreshed my soul. His glorification of Scotland, tempered though it was like that of so many Scotsmen by the enjoyment of English success, was an anchor of hope. Yet except for falling in love with Diana Vernon I was never carried out of myself by any of his great novels. They bored me then, and they bore me even more completely now. Not all the eloquence poured out in 1932 availed to revive Scott as a novelist, and if ever I felt safe in prophesying anything I feel safe in prophesying that he will never be revived in the future.

George Eliot was another novelist whose books our pastors and masters thought we were equipped to read in the tender green of youth, particularly *The Mill on the Floss*. Obstinacy combined with contrariness prevented my ever doing so; but *Romola* made a deep impression which endured until *The Cloister and the Hearth*, read in one of Chatto and Windus's "yellow-backs," obliterated it. Then came the day when lightly and casually my father tossed a volume to me across the table.

"Here," he said, "this is more in your line than mine."

That volume was *Treasure Island*. This was in the year 1890 when I was seven years old, and if some good fairy offered to give me back a few hours of early youth I would choose those hours when I was reading *Treasure Island* for the first time. It is now the fashion to deplore Robert Louis Stevenson's influence and scoff at his work. Partly the reaction was brought about by the indiscriminate raptures of his admirers, especially the American ones, partly by what came to seem Stevenson's attitudinizing morality in his essays—that one on Burns is as pretty a piece of cant as may be found in English litera-ture—but chiefly, I fancy, by the publication of his letters and Grahame Balfour's biography. The tide was already running heavily against him in the years just before the war, and since the war he has drifted off the course for most of the younger writers. Nothing is easier than to build up a critical case against Stevenson that will ensure a verdict of guilty. Nothing is more difficult than to make intelligible to these ruth-less young moderns the spell Stevenson cast upon readers during the last decade of the nineteenth century. It was comparable in its potency to that which Scott had cast seventy years earlier. It may be that were I to be reading Stevenson for the first time to-day I should be as much irritated by him as many of my contemporaries and the great majority of my juniors. Yet I lived through experiences during the war which were comparable in their adventurous quality with anything that Stevenson imagined in books or experienced himself in the South Seas, and if the bulk of Stevenson's writing is really nothing better than romantic fustian I cannot help feeling that I ought to be aware of it nowadays. On the whole I am inclined to suspect the deficiencies of Stevenson's detractors rather than the indiscrimination of his admirers.

The same bitter resentment against a romantic personality is displayed in the current view of Rupert Brooke, and even more unjustly, for if Rupert Brooke's attitude toward war is revolting to those who are only capable of perceiving the sordid and brutal aspects of war, and still more revolting to those who never experienced war at all but have merely gained an idea of it from the ordure and hysteria of *All Quiet on the Western Front*, one cold fact remains, which is that Rupert Brooke died for his country. Many of the present generation regard such a death as an emotional impertinence, for which they find it as hard to forgive Rupert Brooke as for the proclamation in a sonnet of his willingness to die for his country. This point of view is a little bewildering to those who discern a larger dignity and a nobler courage in the self-revelation of R. L. Stevenson or Rupert Brooke than in the puling exhibitionism of certain writers much in vogue and greatly esteemed for their intellectual integrity and moral courage.

Nevertheless, it will not do to attribute entirely the anti-romantic bias so much in evidence at the end of the first third of the twentieth century to a reaction against the upheaval of the Great European War. The war gave an impetus and an added weight to that roller of democracy which was already making itself felt during the first decade of this century. Romance is not fostered by a spirit hostile to the notion that any human creature should receive the least advantage from externals, from what is paradoxically called the accident of birth, from wealth or grace or beauty, or even from a more generous allowance of vitality than is granted to the average man or woman. It is true that the present state of democracy demands individuals capable of sustaining for the mass the illusion of a richer life, and that it rewards such individuals handsomely; but the footballer who supplies his patrons with vicarious exercise, the film-star who supplies them with vicarious passion, and the novelist who supplies them with vicarious adventure of body and mind, now occupy the same position as the gladiators and charioteers of the Roman Empire. The artist whose fulsome reliance upon the favour of a patron shocks our contemporary notions of independence was actually far more independent than the man who earns his livelihood by his ability to delude the public into fancying that he exists for their pleasure. At no period of the world's history was the artist so completely a slave as he is now. That condition of slavery will probably exterminate him at last. Faith in the ultimate destiny of man must be based on the perfectableness of democracy, but it is not a tenet of such a faith that this immensely remote perfection will find the creative imagination still expressing itself in art. A survey of the past compels a recognition of the fact that art, at any rate as we conceive it, may be only an expression of humanity at a certain stage of its development.

Perhaps some of the feeling against Stevenson is inspired by the instinct of the contemporary writer to protect himself. There is evidence of physical degeneration with the added strain upon the mind of modern conditions. The fight that Stevenson put up against ill-health was carried through to the end on the assumption that there was something disgraceful in being a bodily weakling. That earns him no respect from the intellectual of to-day, whose devitalization is the result of material progress. Stevenson appears as a champion of the medieval humanity to which the modern feels superior. His self-confidence is intelligible. Never was the individual so independent of his own physical resources. Even among the most impoverished and wretched of the population the superficialities of existence have been made easier. The tramp will find a better road and better accommodation along that road than his vagabond predecessor of a century ago. A level of comfort is the ideal of the moment. It is claimed that the standard of living has been raised, and those who are inclined to argue that this elevation is an illusion are regarded as sentimental reactionaries. Perhaps they are. Perhaps it does make for an increase in the totality of human happiness that the mother of a household should have the wherewithal to open a tinned tongue for supper and thus leisure to watch Marlene Dietrich or Greta Garbo living as a substitute for herself. We are too near the process to be sure of the ultimate effect. Yet the quality of this substitute existence is discouraging to those who believe that leisure is what is required for mankind to express itself. Aristotle's argument that slavery was necessary in order to provide a certain number of human beings with leisure never foresaw that those for whom he desired leisure would one day be themselves the slaves. The fact is we are striving for leisure without due consideration of the way in which that leisure will be spent. We are confusing it with comfort, or rather we are making them mutually interdependent. In the enjoyment of one the artist flourishes; but in possession of the other he decays.

"Did you ever see Flint's ship?" Squire Trelawney was asked in *Treasure Island*.

"I saw his topsails once off Trinidad," was the answer. "And the cowardly son of a rum-puncheon with whom I was sailing put back into Port of Spain."

It might be excessive to accuse the detractors of the Stevensonian manner of being cowardly sons of rum-puncheons; but in 1933 the mere sight of romantic topsails on the horizon does drive many contemporary writers back into Port of Spain.

At the moment fine writing is regarded with suspicion, and it is supposed that anybody can do it who will condescend to such trickery. Such a theory will not bear examination. The continuity of culture has been broken. Whether it was snapped by the war or worn through by the attrition of material progress does not matter. It may be for the ultimate good of the white race that Latin and Greek should cease to be the cornerstones of their education. That I am not concerned to argue. The immediate result of despising the past has been to let loose upon art a horde of young barbarians who have not yet discovered how to communicate with the greater part of their fellow-men. The position of literature at the moment (and of the other arts also) is the position of religion just after the Reformation. Some believe that the Reformation was necessary, useful, and ultimately fruitful. Others believe that it was not. Few, however, will be bold enough to deny that the achievement of it entailed a good deal of confusion. I do not want to prejudice the argument at this stage by denying the necessity, utility, and ultimate fruitfulness of our literary reformation. I merely wish to emphasize the present stage of confusion. I recognize the destructive accomplishment: the constructive accomplishment is less obvious. None of those who profess to dispose of Stevenson with a sneer is capable of handling the English language with a fraction of his control. That such perfect control should parody itself occasionally was inevitable whenever manner was called upon to conceal lack of matter.

An artist's lack of matter is to some extent a lack chargeable against the time and circumstances in which he is compelled to work. *Weir of Hermiston*, the unfinished book on which Stevenson was working when he died, displays him at his very highest, and, idle though such speculation is, it may fairly be postulated that if death had not cut short his career at the age of forty-four the labour of mastering his craft would have been repaid more richly than time allowed. If Thomas Hardy had died at the age of forty-four he would not have written his four greatest novels. The outbreak of the Boer War would have been a test for Stevenson, and he would only have been sixty-four when the Great War broke out. It is not absurd to believe that he would have survived both tests triumphantly. Nevertheless the admirers of Stevenson must face the fact that his contemporary influence was diffused by his earlier books, and it is easy to sympathize with those who consider that influence to have been deleterious to the vitality of the English novel by the undue importance it attached to what in effect was a mere game of let's pretend. It is impossible to avoid an occasional smile when reading Stevenson's letters to find him seriously concerned about the propriety of his incidents. We find it hard to believe that our grandfathers were really as much overcome as they apparently were in the theatre by what we should laugh at now for rant. Therefore we are inclined to forget that these discussions about the excessively macabre or vicious or passionate upon which Stevenson embarked with critics like Sydney Colvin or Edmund Gosse were genuinely serious discussions, without indulging Stevenson as one might indulge a child by discussing a bad dream of his the night before. It is as well to chasten ourselves when we feel superior to the emotional response of our grandfathers in the theatre or to the anxiety of Stevenson for the nerves and morals of his readers by reflecting upon some of the popular successes in fiction which have infected ourselves with a fever. After an examination of the best-sellers over a hundred years posterity is not likely to laugh with a greater kindliness at our temporary aberrations of taste than at those of our forefathers.

Some of the reaction against Stevenson was caused by those who persisted in carrying on his tradition when it was evidently time for serious writers to confront seriously the problems of contemporary life. Examples of unduly protracted Stevensonianism might be found in the romances of Sir Arthur Quiller-Couch or Mr. John Buchan. Yet, if one is going to quarrel with such writers let us quarrel with what they are doing, not with the way they are doing it. In that case the only logical attitude is the ruthless one which declares that all novels are a waste of time to write and a waste of time to read. For such an attitude there is much to be said, and a remote posterity may laugh at the childishness of ancestors who were able to enter-

tain themselves with deliberately contrived fic-
tions. For my part I am thankful to be living at
a stage in the evolution of humanity when most
of us still possess sufficiently primitive minds to
be able to enjoy a story. I recognize that mere
entertainment is fast ceasing to become the
novelist's privilege owing to the successful competition of what the great mass of the public will
soon consider better entertainment than he can
provide. I recognize too the efforts being made
to carry the novel beyond the story-telling stage
in the hope of its survival in the new age that is
confidently expected to emerge when the full
implications of relativity have been thoroughly
assimilated. Yet I permit myself the pleasure of
doubting whether the novel is not an expression
of time as we have hitherto conceived time, and
whether with the disappearance of that conception the novel will not vanish in its company.

# CHAPTER IV

## DISCOVERING BOOKS FOR ONESELF

PROFITABLE though an occasional recommendation from above might be, such moments as the first reading of *Treasure Island* were rare enough. Our intuition was to distrust the advice of our elders, and it was the unfettered choice of favourite books to which one must look back to discover the more potent influences that early reading provided. The library of which I had the freedom was almost exclusively dramatic, and it is no exaggeration to say that before I was thirteen I had read every play of major or minor importance written and produced by the year 1830. In my mind dialogue and action were thus firmly fixed as the dominant expression of the imagination. The result of reading so many plays of various periods was to free my mind completely from the repressions imposed by Victorian prudery. A boy who knew almost by heart the whole of Congreve and Wycherley could hardly be expected to understand the fuss he heard being made about plays like *The Notorious Mrs. Ebbsmith* or *The Second Mrs. Tanqueray*. By such a boy the meretricious character of Pinero's contribution to English dramatic art was instinctively perceived. He was unable, of course, to put his criticism into words. He had to be content to dismiss as "stupid" what he felt within himself was false, and he had to put up with the attitude of those older than himself who considered themselves bound to assume that plays like *The Second Mrs. Tanqueray* were beyond the comprehension of the young.

The first indication I received that the plays of a century earlier were not regarded by everybody as the ultimate perfection of dramatic achievement was about 1890 when Henry James, who had been to see my father act in *The School for Scandal*, replied on being asked how he had enjoyed the performance:

"A curious old play, a very—curious—old—play!"

And the tone of his voice expressed a kind of painful, indeed of agonized perplexity.

Some time after this Henry James presented his novel *The Tragic Muse* to my father, and having heard that in these three volumes might be found the effect upon the novelist of his late dramatic adventure, the production at the Opéra Comique of the play founded upon his novel *The American*, I set out to read them. Needless to say, at the age of nine I found *The Tragic Muse* incomprehensible and unreadable. About the same time I embarked on a novel lately published by an uncle of my own, and finding that equally unreadable I came to the conclusion that contemporary novels were generically "dry." I was vaguely puzzled by the apparent ability of my elders to read them with interest, and doubtless noted down that ability as another instance of adult eccentricity.

The discouraging effect of *The Tragic Muse* was never completely overcome, and except for some of his short stories I never did succeed in reading Henry James, and I never shall be able to read him. About the date of which I am writing, my father, having occasion to visit the novelist where he was then living in De Vere Gardens, close to Kensington High Street, took me with him, and I remember that while we were waiting for the great man the various desks at which he worked were pointed out to me. There was a desk at which he could write standing, another at which he could write kneeling down, another at which he sat, and unless memory deludes me, a fourth desk at which he wrote lying on his belly. It will be understood how deeply this scrivener's gymnasium impressed upon my youthful fancy the complication of the process known as writing a novel. Beyond the fact that it was a fine morning in early summer, and that Henry James was wearing a dark beard, I recall nothing more of this interview. No doubt he and my father discussed problems of "cutting," for when James had first read *The American* to the company at the Theatre

Royal, Sheffield, the process had lasted six and a half hours!

That was the first time I saw Henry James. The last time I saw him was at his flat in Chelsea in the early autumn of 1914, when, after vainly endeavouring to find some way of achieving active service, I decided to return to Italy and write another book. Henry James asked me what my subject was to be and I told him very briefly the story of *Guy and Pauline*.

"Well, my dear boy," he said, "you have not left me much the wiser at the end of your attempt to gratify my perhaps impertinent curiosity." Then seeing that I was embarrassed by the suggestion of having acted with a wilful *gaucherie* he went on quickly: "But I remember I once asked our beloved George Meredith about a novel on which he was then engaged, and I remember how after an exposition of more extended length and greater complicacy than yours I found myself at the end of it knowing about his new book absolutely nothing at all."

On my way out, when with that so beautifully elaborate courtesy of his he was escorting me to the door of the Chelsea flat, he said, with the evidently kind intention of reassurance in case he should have discouraged me by his reception of the outline of *Guy and Pauline*, that the only time he was able to see his story clearly was in the first full synopsis of it.

"You," he said to me, "have the best gift that any writer of novels can have, which is the ability to receive the direct impact of life so that you can return it directly to your readers. People and things reach me only after glancing from angle to angle all round like tennis balls, and I can only return them to my readers by the same circuitous and indirect method."

That early dislike of mine for novels was strictly limited to contemporary novels. I could not read enough of Smollett and Fielding, particularly of Smollett. *Roderick Random* seemed to me the best book that was ever written, and I must have read it a dozen times before I was thirteen. The second favourite was *Peregrine Pickle*. Smollett's best novel, *Humphrey Clinker*, I cared for less, so one may presume that it was the knockabout life of the first and second which delighted the growing boy. This was equally true of my enjoyment of *Tom Jones*. There was nothing knockabout in *Clarissa Harlowe* and still less of it in *Sir Charles Grandison*. Yet I read both these two long novels without missing a page, and of *Clarissa Harlowe* I read a good deal two or three times over. Nor so far as I can recollect was my reading of it influenced by sexual curiosity. The thrill that girls used to obtain from the surreptitious perusal of *Jane Eyre* was at my disposal in Byron's *Don Juan*, which I already knew almost by heart when after five or six years of reading it a governess, much to my amusement, suggested that *Don Juan* was not suitable reading for a boy of fourteen. She herself was not a Donna Julia.

Another interference with my reading at this date came when it was discovered that I had bought a copy of Henry Cockton's story, *Sylvester Sound*. I do not suppose that anybody now reads *Valentine Vox* and *Sylvester Sound*. At that date they had both been published well over fifty years, but they were still obtainable, paper-bound, at a shilling, and could be found at any stationer's among the piles of cheap reprints. The theme of *Sylvester Sound*, as I remember it, was similar to Bellini's *La Sonnambula*. And who now reads *Frank Fairleigh*? Yet it lingered on as regular reading more than forty years after its first publication. At the time it seemed to offer a wonderful revelation of life as it really was and the promise of a glorious freedom when at eighteen years old that life should be one's own. *Frank Fairleigh* was a novel about life at a private tutor's and at Cambridge, but I fancy it has long passed from the possibility of being read with serious interest. *Verdant Green*, a novel about Oxford life published about the same date, was still to be seen at every bookshop when I went up to the University in 1901, and for all I know it may still be in circulation there to-day. Those who on the strength of a few great names praise the past above the present in fiction will have to admit that the general standard of novel-writing during the second half of the nineteenth century must have been pretty low for novels like those of Cockton and Smedley to maintain themselves in circulation as long as they did. In the 'eighties the English novel had sunk to its nadir. It was indeed almost as negligible as the English drama. William Black, Robert Buchanan, Edna Lyall, David Christie Murray, Margaret Oliphant, John Strange Winter, James Payn—these were the popular novelists of the 'eighties, and not merely popular but esteemed as novelists of literary worth. Of the major novelists Hardy produced two of his greatest books, *The Mayor of Casterbridge* and *The Woodlanders*, and George Meredith produced *The Tragic Comedians* and *Diana of the Crossways*. This is not a conspicuously rich harvest for a whole decade, and when we are inclined to question the reputation awarded to Robert Louis Stevenson we have to remember that during this barren decade he published *New Arabian Nights*, *Treasure Island*, *The Silverado Squatters*, *Prince Otto*, *Dr. Jekyll and Mr. Hyde*, *Kidnapped*, *The Merry Men*, *The Black Arrow*, *The Master of Ballantrae*, and in collaboration *The Dynamiter* and *The Wrong Box*.

Two novels published in the 'eighties which profoundly stirred contemporary opinion were

*Robert Elsmere* by Mrs. Humphry Ward and
*John Inglesant* by J. H. Shorthouse. The former,
which dealt with the difficulties of a clergyman
in accepting supernatural religion, has faded out
of the public mind. The latter, which evoked a
convincing picture of Rome in the seventeenth
century, of Quietism, and of Jesuit intrigue, is
still readable, though some of the credit which
Shorthouse was given for his imitations of
seventeenth-century prose must be discounted
by the discovery that much of it was borrowed
without acknowledgment from seventeenth-
century writers. And now on reflection I
remember that George Moore produced during
the 'eighties *A Modern Lover*, *A Mummer's
Wife*, *A Drama in Muslin*, and *The Confessions
of a Young Man*. It is in these books that we
may perceive more clearly than in any the imminent decay of Victorianism. They are the
first novels in English which show evidence of
an author's awareness of European tendencies,
and they are an attempt to apply the lessons of
Parisian life and Parisian letters to English life
and English letters. These early works of George
Moore are not good novels, for the author's
desire to shock the bourgeoisie is stronger than
his desire to present a view of life unimpeded by
the genteel fogs of puritanism. In the result,
although he avoids a blur, he does not preserve
his perspective. The value of them is not the

picture they present of social life in the 'eighties, but the revelation they afford of what must have been the mental state of society when the intellectual revolt against it was expressed in such novels. The vulgarity of a novel like *A Drama in Muslin* makes it unreadable now, because it adopts an attitude by which to-day we should be surprised in the servants' hall. This is one of the penalties we pay for a class-conscious civilization. Every vulgarity has once been a modishness, or at any rate an assertion of gentility. The good manners of the eighteenth century were characterized by what came to seem an excess of formality, and English good manners to-day are recognized by an apparent absence of any manners at all. Formality lingers in suburban or provincial manners long after it has disappeared from the *milieu* which evolved its rules. In America, or for that matter in Scotland, what seems to people of the world an excessive attention to the use of a prefix like "Mr." prevails. Strangers introduced to one another express their pleasure at the meeting, and nowadays it is considered a demonstration of good-breeding in the ill-bred plutocratic society of to-day to sneer self-consciously at such outmoded ceremonies of speech. The same excessive and elaborate formality lingers in the ballrooms of the provinces. Whether an outlived courtesy deserves the contemptuous mockery of those who believe themselves fashionable is a problem of modern manners. Perhaps when informality has permeated suburban gentility, formality will begin all over again.

What happens to manners happens to words. Corsets replace stays; napkins become serviettes. "Smock" came to sound vulgar, and "shift" was adopted as a genteel substitute. In its turn the genteel substitute became vulgar, and "shift" was replaced by "chemise." "Chemise" in turn degenerated into "shimmy." If the garment were still commonly worn in fashionable society, no doubt with the whirligig of time it would be ruled that it should be called "smock" again. Then the gentility grows too insistent and in its turn acquires the mark of vulgarity. Right through the Victorian age this gentility in the matter of wearing apparel was always asserting itself. The end of the eighteenth century provides an example of this, when an honest word like "breeches" acquires an embarrassing directness for the nice-minded and we find the ridiculous compound "small-clothes" being used. Presently "small-clothes" became too much for a hyper-sensitive age, and by Dickens's time we begin to hear of facetious euphemisms like "inexpressibles" and "unmentionables," or ponderous gentilities like "nether-garments." An age whose pruriency allowed and even demanded of its novelists such circumlocutions was hardly likely, in the words of one of its own poets, to see life steadily and see it whole. The peak of absurdity was reached in America when it became a breach of manners to allude in public to the legs of a table.

"Father is rather vulgar, my dear. The word Papa, besides, gives a pretty form to the lips. Papa, potatoes, poultry, prunes and prism are all very good words for the lips; especially prunes and prism."

With the decade which began in the year 1880 the prunes of the Victorian age were beginning to show signs of blue mould and the prisms were cracking. It was George Moore's destiny to be the writer in English chosen to break some of the taboos. I can distinctly remember that the great sin he committed against propriety in *A Drama in Muslin* was in his making one young woman mention in conversation with another young woman the fact that she was wearing shammy-leather drawers. The printing of the word "drawers" sent a shudder throughout the British Isles. This is not surprising when we remember that the British Isles had only recently managed to endure seeing and hearing the word "trousers." Indeed, many years were to go by before the word "drawers" could be printed as a matter of course, and as recently as 1913 I received several letters of protest from correspondents because I had ventured to print such a suggestive word in a novel of my own. It may be necessary later on in examining the works of more modern novelists to discuss the use of words that have such power to shock upon the printed page, but it is probably true to say that it was George Moore's manner at first rather than his matter which gave him a reputation for being what was and still is infelicitously called a realist writer. In fact, one may go so far as to hazard that it was not until Thomas Hardy followed up *Tess of the D'Urbervilles* with *Jude the Obscure* that the British public really began to wake up to the fact that the niceness of their literature, of which they had been so proud when they remembered the nastiness of the literature on the other side of the English Channel, was being seriously threatened at last.

# CHAPTER V

## GEORGE MEREDITH AND THOMAS HARDY

YET, even so long ago as 1856, a novel which was to possess a profound importance for at least two generations had been considered unfit for circulation in the libraries. That was *The Ordeal of Richard Feverel*. It is difficult now when turning over the pages of a novel by George Meredith to be sure exactly what were the qualities that could bewitch so completely my seventeenth and eighteenth and nineteenth years, and it is even more difficult to understand why at this late date those novels should show signs of becoming the intellectual pets of young France. So far as my inquiries have been able to elicit an answer, the novels of George Meredith seem to be as incapable of making any appeal to the younger generation of Great Britain as they now are to myself. In my own case the reaction against them had already begun when the publication of that injudicious selection of George Meredith's private correspondence revealed what a combination of insincerity, hypocrisy, and intellectual pretentiousness the great man really was. It is strange that he has so far escaped being burnt as a guy by one of those biographical incendiaries who delight in making bonfires of former idols. None of the great Victorians offers such a wealth of inflam-

mable material. I suspect it is due to the pro-
verbial piety which deters dog from eating dog.
The young intellectual of to-day fears to make a
guy of one to whom all intellectuals of a generation
ago bowed down. Such an action might weaken
the infallibility with which the contemporary
intellectual claims to recognize the significant
novelists of to-day. It can hardly be accidental
that in a book published in 1932 by Mrs. Q. D.
Leavis called *Fiction and the Reading Public*,
George Meredith's name is not mentioned.
*Fiction and the Reading Public* is an attempt, and
on the negative side an almost completely successful attempt, to analyse popular taste in the
reading of fiction. Yet the problem of George
Meredith, a solution of which would have
gravely affected the author's theory, was avoided,
and one must suppose deliberately avoided. For
years George Meredith held a position the
supremacy of which was never challenged except
by Philistines. The more obscure he became,
the higher his admirers exalted him.

Yet to-day, the domination that Meredith
exercised over fiction has broken down as completely as the education that Sir Austin Feverel
designed for his son. I find it impossible to
believe that the preposterous household of the
Feverels will ever again become credible, that
the aphorisms of the Pilgrim's Scrip will ever
again seem to possess the wisdom of time itself,

or even that the diversion played upon a penny whistle will ever again serve as an overture to youth's enchanted play. The nurse in *Romeo and Juliet* is still alive, but Mrs. Berry has no more life in her now than some rusty old dressmaker's model in the corner of an attic. *Evan Harrington*, which was once considered an inferior novel, has more life to-day than its predecessor, probably because Meredith's desire to release once and for all what the jargon of the moment would call the complex set up by being the son of a tailor imparted life to his book. *Sandra Belloni* and its sequel *Vittoria* form together an epic of grotesques, and the most grotesque characters of all are those whom Meredith designed as examples of real people to set off against the sentimentalists he thought he was satirizing. Comic characters like Mrs. Chump and Mr. Pole are among the most deplorable in English fiction.

I have never had the heart to spoil my memory of *Rhoda Fleming* by reading it in maturity. To do so and find it fustian would be as sacrilegious as to read through a packet of love-letters written in youth and laugh at one's former self. I and many in my generation with me must have been inspired by the story of Rhoda and Dahlia Fleming with such a sense of the passionate tragedy of life as that with which the story of Jeanie and Effie Deans moved an earlier genera-

tion. By the time I was reading *The Egoist*, Sir
Willoughby Patterne had ceased to be the Every-
man he had seemed to Robert Louis Stevenson
and many others. We must accept the possibility of his seeming a universal type on the
evidence of those who found him such; but by
the beginning of the twentieth century the
foundations on which the edifice of Sir Willoughby Patterne had been built were subsiding
so fast that Sir Willoughby was no longer recognizable as a human being, and his egoism seemed
particular to a class and to a period rather than
general to male humanity.

Perhaps the prime cause of Meredith's failure
to maintain his reputation lay in his treatment
of women. Those splendid creatures who swept
across his pages, the peers as once they seemed
of Beatrice and Portia and Rosalind, were presently to agitate for the vote, and in the course of
that agitation, however splendid the leaders of
women might appear, they did not appear
splendid in the way Meredith had designed for
them. Then when the vote was won and women
stood forth emancipated it became obvious to
the most romantic spectator that they were even
less like Meredith's wonderful women than we
were already beginning to suppose them. Well
may Sir Austin Feverel have noted his expectation that woman would be the last thing civilized
by man, for that was what Meredith in his heart

D

believed. The women of his novels were simply abstractions, and from the first page he wrote to the last he never had the courage to face woman as a reality. Consider the sonnet sequence, *Modern Love*. Consider those letters he wrote about his errant wife.

By 1902, when I was nineteen, the stature of Meredith had begun to diminish slightly, but he was still the standard idol of the young Oxford intellectual. There were few rooms in which one did not see those seventeen crimson volumes of the pocket edition, which, when I saw them last on the shelves of my library, an unconscious irony of arrangement had placed on the top shelf next to the twelve volumes of his first father-in-law, Thomas Love Peacock. By 1902 I was myself the slave of Thomas Hardy, and I well recall that, when at some literary society I rose to argue that Hardy was a greater novelist than Meredith, the house declared itself against me unanimously, indeed refused to take my championship with gravity, regarding it as a piece of preposterous affectation. Not even when the following year saw the publication of the first volume of *The Dynasts* was there the least inclination to accept Hardy as a force in English letters comparable to Meredith. It was a younger brother of Maurice Hewlett who first proclaimed to me the gospel of Hardy's greatness, on a wet blowy evening in the late autumn of 1900, when he had found it as hard to convince me that he was in earnest as two years later I was to find it hard to convince Oxford contemporaries of my own sincerity.

The long old age of Hardy during which he achieved a dignity beyond that of Meredith, gathering fresh laurels with the poems he wrote, whereas the laurels of Meredith in his old age had visibly browned with every letter he sent to the newspapers, was a meet reward by fortune for the critical condescension which had accompanied his middle age. Was it Henry James in a letter to Robert Louis Stevenson who spoke of "poor little Tommy Hardy"? That was the general attitude of the leading critics of literature. Those who give themselves the trouble to look through the reviews of the 'seventies and 'eighties will be astonished to find scant evidence that he was regarded as a greater writer than William Black. To be sure, there was some justification for the attitude taken up, because Hardy certainly did intersperse those masterpieces that he himself called novels of character and environment with the second and third-rate works he called romances and fantasies and novels of ingenuity, thus announcing to his readers that he knew when he was writing with the vitality of genius, and when he was merely writing out of the margin of superfluous talent.

Since Hardy's death there are signs of the

inevitable reaction against the indiscriminate and occasionally excessive laudation which marked the last decade of his life, and even the masterpieces are now seen to hold a certain amount of that alloy of which his novels of ingenuity were entirely compounded. I find from pencil notes at the end of the pocket edition, so suitably bound in maroon beside the crimson of Meredith, that in 1920 I was already suffering from that reaction, and that only *The Mayor of Casterbridge* and *Under the Greenwood Tree* were re-read at that date without splenetic criticism. No doubt in due course most of the human beings of Hardy's novels will moulder to dust, but time cannot destroy the countryside with which that dust will be mingled, and if in an unimaginable future England should have sunk like the lost Atlantis, England might still be conjured back for that unimaginable future by populating the countryside of Thomas Hardy with the people of Jane Austen, for that green world of his must exist in time as imperishably as the blue world of Homer.

# CHAPTER VI

## THE ÆSTHETIC MOVEMENT

THE romanticism that began as a reaction against the barren formalism in which the eighteenth century waned away and drew most of its fire and fever from political revolution was sustained during the nineteenth century, at any rate in England, by the instinct to protest against the industrialism and commercialism which with every fresh decade of material prosperity were closing more surely round the English people. In Scotland romanticism in any form died with Scott, and amid the evidence of wealth's increase on every side of him the Scotsman drugged his romantic impulses with deeper and deeper doses of a sentimentalism that finally sent him maundering to sleep in an enchanted kailyard protected against reality by a dense thicket of bonny brier bushes.

In England the man who individually did most to preserve the romantic attitude was John Ruskin, and although by the date of his death in the last year of the nineteenth century his influence appeared to have evaporated in a cloud of melodious rhetoric, the opinions to which he gave such eloquent expression are actually believed with a warmer fervour of vitality at the present moment than they were during the prime of his renown. I myself first began to read Ruskin at the age of sixteen, and when I look back to that first reading of *Sesame and Lilies* I seem to hear Jehovah's thunder in the mountain tops. That great passage of invective printed in red ink which denounced the cynical destruction of beauty by mankind for the sake of material gain still echoes in my ears. To this day I feel it is a personal reproach that we tunnelled the Clarens shore of Lake Geneva, or that we made of the Alps so many soaped poles in a bear-garden up which we climbed and slid down again with shrieks of delight. That kind of thing may be dismissed nowadays as mere emotive rhetoric. No doubt it is, but when the echoes of such emotive rhetoric still resound we must allow it as much force as some of the emotive rhetoric indulged in by prophets like Isaiah and Jeremiah. Whatever we may feel nowadays about Ruskin's theories of art, whatever we may feel nowadays about the Natural History Museum as architecture, the economic prophecies of John Ruskin are being fulfilled hour by hour, and should the present turmoil of distracted economic theory result in economic calm by adopting the only solution possible, that is the application of Social Credit, we shall find John Ruskin on a higher pedestal than his contemporaries ever found for him, for it was Ruskin's emotive rhetoric which gave many a youth the necessary confidence to maintain the truth of his intuition against what was coming to seem the overwhelming weight against him of material evidence.

The literature of the pre-Raphaelite brotherhood to which Ruskin stood as godfather may seem definitely outside the scope of this book; but the æsthetic movement of the 'eighties was really the fruit of pre-Raphaelitism, and the literary and artistic activity of the 'nineties could not have manifested itself without the æsthetic movement of the previous decade. We are apt to derive our impressions of the æsthetic movement from old volumes of *Punch* or from Gilbert and Sullivan's opera *Patience*. We fancy that æstheticism meant parties of ugly young women in greenery-yallery mock medieval dresses and niminy-piminy young men with cheesy complexions and velvet jackets. The epithet æsthete, which in my time at Oxford was used to cover anything from a predilection for homosexuality to an admiration for Botticelli, still holds its own among the young men of my acquaintance, who now use it almost exclusively as a general synonym for any kind of moral eccentricity, such moral eccentricity being usually expressed by an odd taste in literature and painting. It took a strong personality in my day for the owner of it to hang the walls of his room with prints of early Italian paintings, and one should pay a tribute to the wider toleration and better taste of the young man of 1933 by hastening to add that a love

of Italian pictures nowadays would not necessarily involve the possessor of it in a suspicion
of unnatural vice. Still, the unpleasant concomi-
tants associated with æstheticism in the 'eighties,
and justly as it seemed by the Oscar Wilde case,
have kept for the term æsthete a pejorative significance. The present dichotomy of the undergraduate world is into "hearties" and "æsthetes"; and it is perhaps worth while setting on
record here that the use of the word "hearty"
was originally invented to describe the peculiar
attributes of the undergraduates of Trinity College, Oxford, when the present Bishop of St.
Alban's, Dr. Michael Furse, was the Dean of
Trinity. Legend said that "Mike" Furse made
a habit of intervening in drunken revels toward
twelve o'clock on Saturday night when, after
knocking together the heads of some of the
roisterers, he would warn them that their rowdy
conduct could always be expiated by attendance
next morning at prayer in the college chapel.
Thus the muscular Christianity of Charles
Kingsley became the hearty Christianity of
"Mike" Furse, under whose régime Trinity men
were known as hearty Trindogs, a back-slapping,
cheery association of Rugger roughs who might
get drunk on Saturday night, but who never
failed to attend Matins on Sunday morning.
Now the hearty Trindog of 1903 is merged in
that great body of Oxford hearties who uphold

normal behaviour and inconspicuous tastes against the æsthetes to whose existing catalogue of debased crimes communism has probably been added.

Yet the æstheticism of the 'eighties as I remember it lacked many of the lurid and unpleasant attributes by which it was stigmatized. No doubt the affectation was occasionally painful to the roast-beef variety of Englishman. I remember hearing how, when an aunt of mine, defying stage superstition, had worn a certain shade of green gown in which to play Desdemona, Oscar Wilde had knelt and kissed the hem of her robe to express an appreciation for which he had no words. That must have made the hearty onlookers squirm, but then that had been in the 'seventies, and mere hearsay, though I do remember that at my brother's christening in 1885, before I was two and a half, I was presented with a spray of lilies to hold in my arms at the font. Yet such a slight tribute to decorative behaviour which at the time would have seemed so "utterly utter" would hardly seem an affectation to-day when some "too marvellous" child is dressed up as a Kate Greenaway picture to hold the bride's train. We have at any rate learnt nowadays that the decorative is not necessarily a sinister affectation. Time has brought in his revenges. We still smile at the æsthetic ladies in old volumes of *Punch*; but we laugh aloud at the reinforced posteriors of their fashionable and normal sisters; and let me add that nobody who has not seen his nurse's bustle, a monstrous red half-moon hanging over the bedpost against morning, can really appreciate what hideousness the absurd affectations of æstheticism banished from English life. For me the æsthetic movement, described in *The Oxford Companion to English Literature* as "a movement during the 'eighties of last century in which the adoption of sentimental archaism as the ideal of beauty was carried to extravagant lengths and accompanied by affectation of speech and manner and eccentricity of dress," is associated with reading in the dusk Christina Rossetti's serene and exquisite poems for children in that volume called *Sing Song*, the firelight shimmering on the silken green and presumably æsthetic binding, with paintings of my childish companions in fields of daisies and blow-balls, with visits to elderly painters whose walls glowed with princesses in sea-green velvet gowns and knights in armour riding through autumnal woods, with the enchanted forest of Morris wallpapers, with sunsets in a Broadway garden and children holding lighted Japanese lanterns among the lilies and roses and carnations of Sargent's picture, and with a hundred more such moments that float like rainbow bubbles above the rub-a-dub-dub-soap-and-water of remote childhood. And

if I search for a final outward expression of what
æstheticism has stood for I find it on a July day
in 1903 when I walked across the water meadows
from Lechlade to Kelmscott Manor. Mrs.
William Morris was sitting in a shaded arbour,
huge and swarthy-seeming in a full white dress.
I behold her across the years powerful and mysterious like Sidonia the Sorceress. I remember
that she defied the sun under a great green-lined
gingham umbrella, and in stately fashion led us
up the paved garden path edged with a trim box
border, on either side of which runnels of water
that guarded the flower-beds against slugs ran
purling. It was with the condescension of one
who had lived in elfland that she took us through
the shadowy rooms of the old house that we
might see the paintings for which she had sat as
model to Rossetti and Madox Brown and many
another, that we might see those full lips and
that neck like an ivory tower. The cool house
seemed like a casket of jewels, so rich were the
walls with ardent colour, so beryl-green the lat-
tices. And then I remember, though why or how
his name should have cropped up in these sur-
roundings, that Miss May Morris and myself fell
to discussing the romances of Joséphin Péladan,
in whose Rosicrucian extravagances we discovered a common interest. That the name of
one of the esoteric French writers to whom the
'nineties, searching ever for the strange, the new,

and it must be added the often incomprehensible, had paid homage symbolizes for me the progress one had made from the æstheticism of the 'eighties to the elaborate decadence of the nineteenth century's end. And equally symbolic does it appear to me that shortly after this visit to the house of William Morris I should have read *The Way of All Flesh*, the first publication of which, as I recall, was in the autumn of 1903, for with the publication of Samuel Butler's posthumous novel a fresh world for exploration was offered to curious youth.

*The New Republic* by W. H. Mallock should not be included in this survey, having been published in 1877; but that Platonic symposium up to date conveys such a clear notion of the English intellectual world just before it vanished in the artificially protracted Victorianism of the last fifteen years of the nineteenth century that I cannot resist bringing it back to the public memory. Here in a country house we listen to the discussions of those who can be identified as Huxley, Tyndall, Carlyle, Ruskin, Matthew Arnold, Jowett of Balliol, Walter Pater, Leslie Stephen, Pusey, and W. K. Clifford, and we realize the atmosphere of profound pessimism about the future into which the English intellectual world had sunk after fifty years of scientific and industrial progress more rapid than any previous half-century in history. There are few signs here of

the complacency with which the present credits
the Victorian era, and indeed except for the caricature of W. K. Clifford under the name of
Saunders there is no exponent of confidence in
the future. Mallock's own prejudice undoubtedly
inclined him to accentuate the perplexity of
thought and ambiguity of utterance by which the
symposium is dominated. Nevertheless, it is on
the whole a fair representation of the state of
mind that prevailed, and if the topics discussed
appear at a first glance immensely remote, it
would not strain ingenuity overmuch to discuss
them again in terms of to-day. I commend to
some brilliant young man the task of writing a
still newer Republic in which the persons might
be Sir James Jeans, Sir Arthur Eddington, Mr.
Bertrand Russell, Mr. Bernard Shaw, Mr. G. K.
Chesterton, Mr. H. G. Wells, Mr. Ford Madox
Ford, Sir James Frazer, Mr. Orage, and Mr.
Aldous Huxley.

# CHAPTER VII

TENNYSON died in 1892. To myself at the age
of nine it seemed a world-shaking event when I
saw that some of the daily papers were edged
with black as if for the death of a king. It would
be too much to claim that at nine years old I
was aware that with the death of Tennyson one
of the keystones to the Victorian arch had been
removed. The Queen herself seemed, as I look
back to my mental outlook then, bound to live
for ever. I had just had a personal encounter
with her at the corner of Russell Road near
Addison Road railway station. I had seen the
royal carriage come sweeping along from the
direction of Hammersmith heralded by two
scarlet outriders. A stone had lodged in the
shoe of one of the horses, and the carriage had
pulled up close to the kerb to allow a scarlet-
coated footman to jump down from the box
and, I suppose, make use of that instrument
attached to many-bladed pocket-knives in those
days to extract stones from horseshoes. There
seem to be no passers-by as I look back on the
scene. I am standing alone on the pavement
being bowed to by a little old lady in black
whom I recognize as the Queen, and to whom
I bow back gravely time after time until the footman jumps on the box. Then the carriage sweeps

on in the direction of that palace where fifty-five years earlier she had been wakened early on a June morning to be hailed as Queen of England, the little old lady in black herself still bobbing and bowing on the air-cushion which provided the automatic movement to acknowledge the salutations of her subjects. An encounter like that added for the imagination of a child the fancy of her omnipresence to her apparent immortality. Eight long years of youth, as long seeming in retrospect as they must have been in reality, were still to drag by before the Queen died and the Victorian age came officially to an end. Indeed, the little boy who had this personal encounter with that mighty old lady was to be old enough to receive the Queen's Commission before the Victorian age was succeeded by that mythical Edwardian age so dear to the facile label-writers of to-day.

Yet it was with the death of Tennyson in 1892 that Victorianism as an active principle expired, and I can well remember that as a result of the delay in appointing a new poet laureate we in youth were left with the definite impression that poets were as extinct as Large Copper butterflies. The schoolboy of fourteen is usually a representative of popular opinion, and at this date the popular mind had forgotten, now that the excitement of *Poems and Ballads* had long since died away, that such a poet as Swinburne was still alive. When in 1896 Lord Salisbury at last made Alfred Austin poet laureate it was considered the final proof of poetry's extinction. Forty-two years of Tennyson and thirty-seven years before them of Wordsworth and Southey had dimmed the disgrace of the eight poet laureates who preceded them: Shadwell, the first of that discordant octave, being appropriately chosen by Dutch William to supersede the great and glorious Dryden.

There were plenty to declare that Tennyson himself was nothing more than a metrical version of the Albert Memorial. There were some who vowed that great poetry had died with Shelley. That may become an accepted opinion in due course. Tennyson and Browning, the two major poets of the second half of the nineteenth century, show no signs at present of ever recovering the position they once occupied either in popular or critical estimation, and it would be idle to pretend that time has produced any major poet of comparable grandeur since. Keats, when he decided to leave *Hyperion* as a fragment, had divined the inevitable collapse of major poetry under the strain of the material development of the white races, and his premature death may be held to have robbed literature of more great prose than great verse.

The failure of Browning to impress the world of to-day to the extent that his devotees confidently expected from posterity is probably due to the recognition that so much of his verse is bad prose and that so much of his apparently subtle profundity and psychological originality is the result of shirking the greater clarity which prose would have demanded. Perhaps after all he was essentially a minor poet even although the externals were those of major poetry. I count as minor poetry that in which the need for particular expression exceeds the need for general comprehension. There is no space here for an argument about poetics, and I only ask readers to accept that definition as one which is temporarily convenient in order to make it clear that in distinguishing between major and minor poetry I am not attempting to establish a comparative value between them. With the incontestable decline of major poetry a just estimation of minor poetry becomes more difficult, for we have now reached a point when the minor poet appears to absolve himself from any responsibility at all for the communication of his utterance. That opens a way to charlatan critics who exploit the esoteric qualities of a poet's work and play the witch-doctor to the taste of the majority. Obscurity has always been a privilege of minor poets, but during the last fifty years that privilege has been increasingly abused.

We shall probably be right in saluting Edgar Allan Poe as the first authentically modern poetic

E

voice, and we shall certainly find in Poe's literary criticism the earliest expression of the contemporary æsthetic attitude. Poe's influence on European poetry was not exerted directly. It was diffused through Baudelaire, and it should be noted that Baudelaire's discovery of Poe did not, as is commonly supposed, suggest to Baudelaire a theory of poetry to which he later gave a personal expression, but that it revealed to him the contemporaneous existence on the other side of the Atlantic of a twin soul. The direct influence of Poe on English literature was never, so far as my reading goes, perceptible, and even in the 'nineties, by which time the French symbolist poets who were the successors of Baudelaire were shattering all the conventional æsthetic ideas, the poetry of Poe himself was regarded primarily as the expression of a sterile ingenuity rather than as a profoundly significant shadow of the future. That ruthless analysis by Poe of the composition of *The Raven*, which, could it have been digested by English criticism, would have cleared away so many fogs, was regarded as the bravado of affectation. Snobbery may have lain at the root of this attitude. Not even the enthusiasm of Baudelaire could persuade the elect that a poem like *The Raven*, which shared a place with *Eugene Aram* in the repertory of popular reciters, deserved their homage.

The poems of the French symbolists were another matter. No young man in the literary fashion could afford to let his bookshelf remain empty of Charles Morice's anthology of modern French poetry, which included Charles Morice's beautifully incomprehensible introduction. In that anthology was to be found Arthur Rimbeaud's sonnet on the vowels which begins: *A noir, E blanc, I rouge, U vert, O bleu.* That was the bugle-call at the summons of which we charged against Philistia. My own view of the 'nineties may be coloured by the fact that they coincided with my 'teens, on which that sense of life awakening from the snores of latter-day Victorianism cast an intoxicating spell. Like everybody else I was convinced that we were the spectators of a rich sunset, and we were thus entirely free from that self-conscious heraldic attitude which made the years just before the Great War seem a little blatant in comparison.

Actually, of course, the 'nineties, far from being a sunset, were a sunrise, and to regard them as anything else is as absurd as to regard the French Revolution as a political sunset and to find the political sunrise in Chartism. Much of the discredit which has been cast upon the 'nineties is due to their apparent preoccupation with naughtiness. The now emancipated young modern finds it difficult to understand what strikes his habituated mind as an excessive and insincere kind of inverted Jack Hornerism. To him the figures of the 'nineties appear to be continually pulling out plums and telling the world what bad boys they are. It is true that there was a great deal of this plum-pulling, but some allowance must be made for the years of inhibition which had preceded what now seems such an exaggerated proclamation of libertinage. Psycho-analysis had not arrived to provide a convenient sink for waste morals, and the concept of sin was still in the minds even of those who, as they would have said in the 'nineties, had lost their faith in the Christian revelation. Works like Kraft-Ebbing's *Psychopathia Sexualis*, written in Latin, and the researches of Havelock Ellis along the by-ways of sexual eccentricity were read by comparatively very few men and still fewer women, while even those that read them acquired little more than statistical information. It was felt that people who behaved oddly and devoted their affections to unusual objects were probably mad. There was no theory to account for such madness. Therefore when a reader recognized one of his own vagaries in a case provided by Mr. Havelock Ellis, unless he was willing to accept the proposition that he was mad, he was left with the only alternative of being a sinner. The incubus of puritanism which had lain so heavily and so long upon the peoples of England and Scotland might suggest an explanation for this linking up of an æsthetic revolt with an excessive consciousness of sin, if the mental process were not equally conspicuous across the Channel. Verlaine's alternating moods of emotional piety and equally emotional sensuality are more extreme than any expression of them in English verse. Whatever the cause, an examination of the minor poetry produced during the 'nineties betrays a preoccupation with the decorative aspects of sin which later developments of psychology have caused to seem more trivial and insincere than it really was.

It is difficult when reading a poet like Francis Thompson to acquit him of a deliberate literary pose which we should never dream of imputing to a poet like Richard Crashaw. We have in the lives and writings of the great Spanish mystics and in the paintings and architecture of the seventeenth century evidence of the fervour with which the counter-Reformation could inspire those who surrendered to its fierce vitality. But there was no movement in contemporary England or for that matter in contemporary Europe which could display Francis Thompson as a prime example of its power. He is a stray spark from a conflagration which had burnt itself out two centuries before he was born. The overladen rococo of Crashaw's English too often becomes in Thompson's hands what seems the

deliberate affectation of a faith hiding its unreality in superfluous and meaningless ornamen-
tation. Yet, while we may admit that he clogged
his genius by using an outlived medium, it is
impossible to read *The Hound of Heaven* without
recognizing in it a sincere and authentic expression of a man haunted by religion and unable to
adjust himself to the destructive forces that were
let loose upon the world when human ingenuity
had begun to move too fast for human powers of
adaptability. The mundane crisis which such a
manner of progress has brought about in the
year 1933 was already apprehended in the
'nineties as a contingency. Looking back at that
period now, we should be able to discern in it a
miniature of the state of the world to-day, and
it is only if we regard the literature of the
'nineties as a forerunner of literature to-day and
not as a coloured footnote to the literature of
yesterday that we can hope to appreciate the significance of that exciting decade.

I shall be bold enough to claim that as a pre-
cocious boy in that decade I was better able to
apprehend the life-giving quality of the ambient
intellectual air than those who were actually in
their prime of productive energy, and certainly
better able than those who looking back at its
externals from the present can see in it nothing
more than an interlude played in the not too dim
past before life was as real as it became after the

Great War. I hope there are some schoolboys of fourteen now who are experiencing the intellectual ecstasy which was to be experienced by the schoolboy of 1897 when beneath the huge pomp of the Diamond Jubilee he discerned the old world crumbling. I recall from the mid-'nineties one schoolfellow older than myself actually, but at fifteen or sixteen still in Etons and displaying no hint externally of his real age, a small and handsome Jew, to whom as a kindred spirit I was presented by another brilliant youth two years younger than myself. Three boys of twelve, fourteen and sixteen are wandering across the great green expanse of the St. Paul's playing-fields, and I can recall how the eldest spoke with an enchanting gravity words of prophetic wisdom, in the course of which I was, as you might say, converted to divine the change that was coming. That boy was Leonard Woolf, and when I occasionally feel sceptical about progress, and when I feel inclined to let my reactionary prejudices harden into an immovable negative, I try to recapture that abundant sense of life which made nothing seem impossible upon that green playground not far from forty years ago, and in recapturing the memory of it I regain an assurance of life's purpose. It is hard without a suggestion of sentimentalization to re-conjure an episode like this which by its very nature possesses that dreamlike quality of importance to him who experienced it, but which is, like a dream, ultimately incommunicable. And the reader may well ask what bearing in any case such a reminiscence has upon the business in hand, since a similar experience must have happened to many schoolboys year after year back through time. My only reply can be that in the previous decade of the 'eighties I do not believe three schoolboys could have been filled with such a sense of a collapsing past, such an awareness of an incommensurable future.

# CHAPTER VIII

## "THE YELLOW BOOK"

THE first evidence that any knowledge of what was happening to literature on the Continent had reached England was the publication at Oxford of a magazine called *The Spirit Lamp* as early as 1891. In the early numbers great fun was made of symbolist poets of whom nobody in England had yet heard. It might be too much to claim that *The Spirit Lamp* by laughter began the "decadent" cult at Oxford, and yet it would not be so far from the truth. Here I must digress for a while to discuss the word "decadent."

Some time in the early 'eighties a group of young Frenchmen which included Maurice Rollinat and Edmond Haraucourt, following the French fashion of group formation, of which the Parnassians had hitherto been the most successful example, decided to call themselves Hydropaths, and impose their notions upon the world of art. Presently, in the French manner, they left their headquarters and enlarged their society by frequenting the Café François Premier in the Boulevard St. Michel, where they were joined by Jean Moréas, Charles Morice, Laurent Tailhade, and others. They then dropped the name "Hydropaths" and called themselves "Décadents." Later on Moréas invented the designation "Symbolistes," after which a few of the group seceded and retained the name "Décadents." Largely through J. K. Huysmans' novel *À Rebours*, which had a considerable literary influence on Western Europe, the decadent that Des Esseintes the principal character of the book delighted to think himself became a generic term and wide enough to include every manifestation of *fin-de-siècle* art that struck popular taste as new and strange. Even now the tendency is to think of the peculiar characteristics of the 'nineties as decadence, and this has helped to rob them of their rightful position as heralds of the new age rather than as pall-bearers of the old. To this "decadent" movement in literature attached themselves many of those who had been caught by the æsthetic movement of the 'eighties. Among these was Oscar Wilde, between whom and the French "décadents" there was no kind of intellectual or æsthetic link, but whose persistent flair discovered in the designation a usefully conspicuous label for himself.

Early in the 'nineties Lord Alfred Douglas went up to Oxford and bought *The Spirit Lamp* from the original founders, who included A. C. Philimore, later to become Professor of Latin at Glasgow University, and one of the rare cultural influences in latter-day Scottish University life.

*Many a mad magenta minute*
*Lights the lavender of life:*

Sandys Wason had sung in one of the first numbers of *The Spirit Lamp* in a delicious parody of advanced French æsthetic theories. When Lord Alfred Douglas assumed the editorship, the character of *The Spirit Lamp* changed; it became a serious organ of æsthetic propaganda. Lord Alfred Douglas was himself a poet of the highest promise, and some of his most beautiful poems appeared in his own magazine. An examination of these later numbers of *The Spirit Lamp* reveals very little of what we should now consider decadent in morals or manners or literary style. The extravagant legends which still persist of the 'nineties at Oxford are evidence, if such extravagance can be accepted as evidence, not of decadent morals, but of æsthetic high spirits. That an undergraduate should have vexed the gravity of dons by leading a lobster on a blue ribbon up the High would hardly have been accepted once upon a time as an omen of the destruction of Sodom and Gomorrah. Anybody who visited Oxford in the early 'twenties of this century could have remarked, had his prejudices inclined him that way, far more blatant evidence of a general decadence in morals than he could ever have derived from a visit during the 'nineties.

When with the departure of Lord Alfred Douglas *The Spirit Lamp* ceased to burn, the whole new æsthetic movement still called "decadent" was gathered together in *The Yellow Book*, a quarterly magazine the prestige of which had not been attained since *The Quarterly Review* was produced in the heyday of Edinburgh as a mother of literature. It should be noted that Henley's *National Observer* died in the April of that year 1894 which saw the first number of *The Yellow Book*, and the failure of the public to support such an organ of fierce conservative criticism is significant indeed. When the following year *The New Review* was re-started by William Heinemann and George Wyndham, Henley became editor, and by an ironical stroke the first number contained an obituary notice of Robert Louis Stevenson and the first instalment of *The Time Machine* by an unknown young writer called H. G. Wells.

An examination of the first five numbers of *The Yellow Book* shows that in spite of the "decadent" cover design by Aubrey Beardsley and the inclusion in the index of one or two names associated with the "advance" of literature, most of the contents were contributed by established writers like Bernard Shaw, Henry James, Edmund Gosse, and others of such calibre. Of course Bernard Shaw was esteemed "advanced"; but he was by this date nearly forty, and it would have been a bold man that

would have ventured to call him "decadent."
At that date he was regarded by the Philistine*
as an eccentric music critic and as an even more
eccentric dramatic critic, one of those Johnnies
who cracked up that fellow Ibsen. To be sure,
he had published two or three bad novels which
neither won nor deserved much esteem, but such
plays as he had written had only been staged for
special audiences. The first volume of them,
*Plays Pleasant and Unpleasant*, was not published until 1898, when Shaw was forty-two.
He had been a contributor to *The National
Observer*, but his socialism had been too much
for the policy of that paper.

Contemporaneous with the decadent movement was the realist movement seeming somewhat *après la bataille* when one remembered that
the Goncourts were producing their best work
before the Franco-Prussian War. George Moore
after his first essays in the 'eighties published in
the *annus mirabilis* 1894 *Esther Waters*, which
was followed in 1895 by Thomas Hardy's *Jude
the Obscure*, the two novels demonstrating incontestably the ability of English novelists to
challenge French novelists on their own ground.
*The Yellow Book* did far more for realism than

---

* "Lowbrows" and "highbrows" had not been heard of
in England at that date. British writers visiting America
just before the Great War, of whom I was one, brought
them back in their luggage and put them into current speech
over here.

for decadence, and the peculiar qualities of that aspect of the 'nineties were better served by *The Savoy*, a periodical published under the editorship of Arthur Symons.

But the English novel was looking up in every direction during the first half of the 'nineties. In 1893 E. F. Benson's *Dodo*, with his portrait of what gossip said was Miss Margot Tennant, had made people wonder if good Queen Victoria was still upon the throne. In the same year Sarah Grand had published *The Heavenly Twins*, popularizing for the first time the theme of feminine emancipation. In 1894 appeared two volumes by Anthony Hope, *The Prisoner of Zenda*, which started Ruritanian romance, and *The Dolly Dialogues*, which revolutionized the writing of polite dialogue in novels. In the same year Mrs. Caffyn, under the pseudonym of Iota, published *A Yellow Aster*, which had seemed one of the most daring English novels yet written until in the following year Grant Allen shook the world of morality with *The Woman Who Did*. No wonder Miss Marie Corelli spent 1894 writing *The Sorrows of Satan*. What old-fashioned people considered the sentimentalization of sin was *à la mode*.

And then upon a literary world preoccupied with sin in all its aspects, a world that was rejecting every day more and more of the puritanical prejudices and hypocrisies and pre-

tences which had made Thackeray's preface to
*Pendennis* and his treatment of Becky Sharp
begin to sound so absurd, came with a crash the
prosecution of Oscar Wilde. Looking back at
that case now, I am inclined to say that the effect
of it following upon the introduction of the
pneumatic tyre for safety bicycles and the consequent liberty that the bicycle gave to women
did more to destroy the Victorian idea than anything else. I see myself as if it were yesterday
crossing Piccadilly Circus and being nearly run
over by one of those old green Atlas omnibuses
on which the driver sat under a big umbrella
with favoured passengers on either side of him
as in the old coaching days. I was nearly run
over because I had turned my head away from
the direction of Regent Street in order to read
a *Pall Mall Gazette* placard waved by an excit-
able newsboy who was shouting in a shrill voice,
"Libel action by famous author against well-
known peer! Verdict!" Even to a boy of twelve
that sounded exciting. As a result of that verdict Oscar Wilde was arrested in the Cadogan
Square Hotel, and the deplorable case took its
course. In those days newspapers were not
printed for family reading; they were father's
possession, and father was presumed to be able
to read in his newspaper without blushing what
read in a book would have made him explode
with outraged pudor. We nice moderns who are

inclined to deprecate the devotion and care with which *The News of the World* collects every Sunday morning for the edification of the tired working-man the sexual offences of the previous week, have forgotten the freedom that the Press allowed itself in the days before Mr. Alfred Harmsworth revolutionized journalism by producing a paper which could be read not merely by father but by the rest of the family. *The Daily Mail* was still a year away from birth when the Oscar Wilde case was being fully reported in the papers without any attempt even to soften details that printed in a book would have sent the author and publisher to gaol. Newspapers were cheap, and no amount of care by father to keep them out of the children's reach availed to preserve the innocence of the younger generation. We knew every detail of the case, and there were very few young people who, when Oscar Wilde was sentenced to two years' hard labour, did not feel, whether they were capable of expressing what they felt or not, that there was something wrong with a civilization which attributed so much importance to an eleventh commandment, *Thou Shalt Not be Found Out*. Not that there was any open sympathy with Oscar Wilde. The shock to respectability was too great. Self-righteousness had to be glutted first, and what a glut it wallowed in!

*The Importance of Being Earnest* was running at

the time, and I well remember seeing on my way to school the name of Oscar Wilde on the play-bills, pasted over with a slip of blank paper to protect the purity of the passer-by. Thus did the management of the St. James's Theatre reconcile the claims of God and Mammon. About that time the double collar which we have all been wearing for many years came into fashion. Rumour ascribed its invention to Oscar Wilde. The instinct of the English for comic depreciation called these collars "Ocky" collars, and it was only by slightly altering the shape and doing away with the original V in the front that the fashion was saved. Another modish get-up at that date was a dark-blue serge suit with red tie either of knitted silk or a kind of flannel. Rumour said that this combination was a secret mark by which one epicene made himself known to another, and that fashion died.

Nevertheless, a criminal prosecution for homo-sexuality lent a romantic glamour to the offence. England has always been a stronghold of homo-sexuality, and how far English Common Law is responsible for that is a debatable point. At any rate, if one thing is certain it is that it tends against the interests of public morals to make martyrs of the subjects. This was a lesson that might have been learnt in the Middle Ages when Edward II was murdered in a revolting way because his homosexuality interfered with his

F

politics, and when after death his body, having been taken to Gloucester, became for some time a miracle-working shrine. William Rufus, Richard II, James I and VI, and William of Orange were all homosexual. We read at school "*formosum pastor Corydon ardebat Alexim,*" and it took more than the wit of the average form-master to persuade us that the glowing verb *ardere* merely meant a kindly interest in the beautiful Alexis. We were perfectly prepared to believe that morally we ought to be superior to emotions like Corydon's; but when the bad behaviour of schoolboys became a criminal offence for which they could be sent to gaol as they thought, then bad behaviour at school became a magnificent fashion. The result was that indulgence in it became a mark of intellectual pre-eminence, and if at the present day sane and normal men are shocked by the increase in avowed homosexuality they may look back to the Oscar Wilde case as the impetus to such a state of affairs.

The immediate result of the Oscar Wilde case was to convince the Philistine public that the new art and literature which they had suspected of being immoral because it was unfamiliar was in very fact even more immoral than they had supposed. A foolish and artificial book like *The Picture of Dorian Gray* seemed corrupt enough to have been written by Satan himself. *Inten-*

He prefers Ohnet's novels to all the symbolists, and Mascagni's *Cavalleria Rusticana* to all Wagnerians and to Wagner himself; he enjoys himself royally over slap-dash farces and music-hall melodies, and yawns or is angered at Ibsen; he contemplates gladly chromos of paintings depicting Munich beer-houses and rustic taverns, and passes the open-air painters without a glance. It is only a very small minority who honestly find pleasure in the new tendencies and announce them with genuine conviction as that which alone is sound, a sure guide for the future, a pledge of pleasure and of moral benefit. But this minority has the gift of covering the whole visible surface of society, as a little oil extends over a large area of the surface of the sea. It consists chiefly of rich educated people, or of fanatics. The former give the *ton* to all the snobs, the fools, and the blockheads; the latter make an impression upon the weak and dependent and intimidate the nervous. All snobs affect to have the same taste as the select and exclusive minority, who pass by everything that once was considered beautiful with an air of the greatest contempt. And thus it appears as if the whole of civilized humanity were converted to the æsthetics of the Dusk of the Nations.*

Let us see how Dr. Nordau developed his thesis. In the first place he had a pathetic belief in the finality of the work of such men as Cesare Lombroso, who, it will be remembered, had sought to establish persistent physical characteristics for lunatics and criminals. Later examination of such theories showed that Lombroso's scientific method was no more to be relied upon than phrenology; it contained a certain amount

* By kind permission of Messrs. William Heinemann, Ltd.

of truth, but the particular cases did not in their
totality supply a warrant for the generalizations
to which he rashly committed himself.

> Degenerates are not always criminals, prostitutes,
> anarchists, and pronounced lunatics; they are often
> authors and artists. These, however, manifest the
> same mental characteristics, and for the most part
> the same somatic features, as the members of the
> above-mentioned anthropological family, who satisfy
> their unhealthy impulses with the knife of the assassin
> or the bomb of the dynamiter, instead of with pen
> and pencil.
> Some among these degenerates in literature, music,
> and painting have in recent years come into extra-
> ordinary prominence, and are revered by numerous
> admirers as creators of a new art and heralds of the
> coming centuries.

Thus early did Dr. Nordau commit himself
to a half-truth. The degenerates indicted were
treated under three main headings: Mysticism,
Egomania, and Realism. One was a little taken
aback to find that the first signs of European
degeneration and exhaustion were noted in
England as early as the third and fourth decades
of the nineteenth century with the beginning of
the Oxford Movement, the centenary of which
is being celebrated in this year of 1933. Degeneration showed itself with continually increasing violence in the founding of the pre-
Raphaelite Brotherhood, and the very delirium
of degeneration was reached with Ruskin! Pre-
Raphaelitism becomes Symbolism in France and

Æstheticism in England. Verlaine provides as
many examples of "mental debility" as Swinburne and Rossetti. After Verlaine, Stéphane
Mallarmé and Jean Moréas are then attacked as
leaders, and we find a poet like Jules Laforgue, who
has had a profound influence on contemporary
literature, dismissed as one of a troop of minor
Symbolists. When the Symbolists have been
disposed of, Tolstoism is attacked as a mental
aberration, and no sooner are Tolstoi and Tolstoism disposed of than Wagner is found to be
equally degenerate. It is delicious to read of
Wagner that "his weakness in melodic creation
had struck all impartial musicians." The sec-
tion on Mysticism is brought to a culmination
by what Nordau calls "the idiotic drivelling
of Maeterlinck." Egomania gives Nordau an
opportunity to dispose of Théophile Gautier,
Catulle Mendès, Théodore Banville, and of
course Baudclaire. Their elimination from
serious literature is followed by the elimination
of Villiers de l'Isle-Adam, Barbey d'Aurevilly,
J. K. Huysmans, Maurice Barrès, and Oscar
Wilde. Strangely enough, Dostoievsky comes
in for Nordau's approval, presumably because
he had only read *Crime and Punishment* in an
inadequate German translation. Otherwise Dostoievsky would surely have provided him with
just the evidence he wanted for his theory.

Ibsen and Nietzsche provide material for the

main attack on Egomania, and Nordau's full analysis is worth studying by modern critics in order to make themselves aware of the mental darkness that the writers of the last twenty years of the nineteenth century were condemned to illuminate. The tendency of the moment to suppose that it was not until after the Great War that modernity in its present connotation began requires severe correction. Nietzsche provided Nordau with exactly what he wanted, because Nietzsche's madness could not be contradicted, and he winds up his indictment with these words: ". . . it still ever remains a disgrace to the German intellectual life of the present age, that in Germany a pronounced maniac should have been regarded as a philosopher and have founded a school."

Zola and Edmond de Goncourt provide the chief examples of degeneration cited under Realism.

In spite of the extravagance of most of Nordau's premises and in spite of the absurdity of most of his conclusions there is a modicum of truth in his indictment. Where he goes hopelessly wrong is in his attempt to make the state literature had reached in the last decade of the nineteenth century a dead end. What he diagnosed as a condition of decay was, in fact, the development imposed upon literature by the development of everything else. He perceived the fallacy of his case, but tried to cover it up by attributing the process of degeneration entirely to the top. The lower and the middle classes, except for a few snobs, arrivists, and charlatans who existed by the flattery of exclusiveness, were according to him as sound as ever. This drove him into a ludicrous prognosis of the twentieth century in which painting, literature and music were to be rescued for normality by a simple proletariat and a sane bourgeoisie. How these saviours of culture were to carry forward the grand tradition of the Muses equipped with nothing better than an ability to enjoy the novels of Georges Ohnet and beer-house chromolithographs Nordau did not attempt to suggest. However, positive criticism was not his strong point. When commiserating with England on the disgrace of pre-Raphaelite art and literature he took the opportunity to congratulate her on the fortunate possession of a great poet like Tennyson able to keep the parts sound. Yet Tennyson was every bit as vulnerable as Rossetti or Swinburne or William Morris by the particular methods he used to attack them. Unfortunately for Nordau's theory the development of literature during the twentieth century so far has been on the very lines he had suggested could lead nowhere. A superficial psychopathist might sit down to-day and write another *Degeneration*, finding all the examples

he wanted under Mysticism, Egomania, and
Realism from writers who were still children
when the first *Degeneration* was written. Many
of the psychologists and alienists cited by
Nordau to support his contentions have been
superseded, but a new horde of mental theorists
has taken their place with the help of Freud,
Jung, Adler, and a score of others. He would be
a poor advocate who could not prove that most
of my confrères were fit for a madhouse.

Nordau's work is now, of course, completely
discredited, and it might be urged with a good
deal of justice that it is receiving in this book an
entirely disproportionate amount of attention
so late in the day. My answer would be that
*Degeneration* possesses a far greater value to-day
than it possessed when it was written, for pre-
cisely the same dangerous inability to perceive
the significance of what we call highbrow literature vitiates the normal man's judgment now,
and at the same time vitiates a great deal of
highbrow criticism itself. Nordau's *Degeneration* serves, in fact, as a reminder of horrid
menace to lowbrow and highbrow alike. It is
true that some of the stones which the Philistine
builder rejected have become the heads of
corners; but it is equally true that several
beautiful corner-stones which were apparently
securely placed for ever are now lying about in
the rubbish of time's quarry.

# CHAPTER X

## MEDIEVALISM

IT was noted above that Nordau discovered the first signs of European degeneration, which he attributed to the mental exhaustion consequent upon industrial effort, in the religious revival of the English Church known as the Oxford Movement; and in the medievalism of the pre-Raphaelite he discerned an extension of this decay. However, being, like most Germans, completely incapable of understanding the English character his explanation of the phenomenon was wide of the mark. In the first place, the mental exhaustion caused by industrialism could hardly have been acute as early as 1833. The Oxford Movement was a spiritual revival inspired by the gross lethargy and materialism into which the English Church had sunk, a lethargy and materialism which had driven Wesley out of the fold and which the Evangelical revival of round about 1820 had lacked the force to master. That materialism had culminated in a base alliance with the landlords to promote the iniquitous and insane enclosures.

The real appeal of the Oxford Movement was to a fundamental dissatisfaction at the back of the Englishman's nature. There will always be a large number of Englishmen who will look back to the Middle Ages with regret, because England

never was, is not now, and never will be a
genuinely Protestant country. If one regards the
havoc that Calvinism has made of art in Scotland
and Wales and compares that destructive power
with its utter impotence to affect English art,
such a contention should be obvious without
indulging in theological argument. Let it be
further noted that every revolt against puritan
domination was popular and aristocratic, and
that every impetus toward whiggery, puritanism,
or whatever else you choose to call it, was given
by that part of the nation whose apparently pre-
ponderant influence led Napoleon into calling
it a nation of shopkeepers. The final failure of
Papalism in the reign of Queen Mary was due
paradoxically to the gloomy and puritan aspects
of her Catholicism. Nothing could be more fan-
tastically out of keeping with the true spirit of
Geneva than the Elizabethan era.

Gradually, the English imagination began to
conceive the time before the Reformation as a
golden age. Medievalism, whether linked up
with the religious life of the Anglican Church or
not, possessed a spiritual influence. The legend
of the Holy Grail spoke more deeply to many
English hearts than the Israelitish lore on which
the puritan domination had compelled them to
nourish their romance. The concubines and
cattle of the biblical patriarchs provided a lus-
cious sign of God's favour to the commercial

middle-class that had ousted the yeomen of England, but it had failed to inspire the rest of the country. What had endeared Sir Walter Scott to Englishmen had been *Ivanhoe*, not *Waverley*. So late as 1898 a romance like *The Forest Lovers* of Maurice Hewlett was capable of bewitching thousands of readers. I read it again the other day and was delighted to find that it had kept all its old magic. Later Hewlett took to writing novels of contemporary life, and he was one of those who helped to make the Meredithian manner intolerable to the rising generation. Then he wrote his *Song of the Plow*, in which he celebrated Hodge, the agricultural labourer, from the time of the Norman Conquest. It is a noble poem and deserves a wider fame and deeper gratitude than it has received.

No amount of romantic or sentimental medievalism was enough to lay the bugbear of Popery. That remained and would probably continue to remain a political menace; but when Catholic emancipation was secured and the country appeared not a penny the worse, people did not hesitate to respond to the richer ecclesiastical life that was foreshadowed by the Oxford Movement. There was opposition, of course, and the history of the Anglican Church from 1833 through the nineteenth century was a history of ecclesiastical battles. Queen Victoria, Disraeli,

and *Punch* fought back to back to save the
Anglican Church from the Scarlet Woman, and
no doubt their religious fervour was to some extent fanned by the fact that Mr. Gladstone was
a High Churchman. Now, although there was
no direct connection between the medievalism
fostered by William Morris or Ruskin and the
medievalism that was being fostered by Dr.
Pusey and his successors, there is no doubt that
the growth of Ritualism, Anglo-Catholicism, or
whatever it may be called by supporters and
opponents, did promote a state of mind that
welcomed the kind of art and literature diffused
by the pre-Raphaelites and their literary heirs.
The religious and the artistic development moved
on parallel lines in the same direction, and they
were the manifestations of a similar disposition
of mind. It is therefore significant that when
puritanism had secured that glorious triumph
over æstheticism in the Oscar Wilde case, it
should immediately afterwards have launched a
desperate attack on what it called the "Roman-
isers" in the Church of England. Having succeeded in discrediting "æsthetic" art, it aimed
to discredit "æsthetic" religion.

The year 1898 was marked by what the Press
called "the crisis in the Church of England."
This is not the place to chronicle that business at
length, but it should be observed that many of
the Roman Catholic novelists and poets promi-

nent to-day spent one of their most impressionable years of youth as Anglo-Catholics in 1898.

My own share in the crisis in the Church of England at the age of fifteen was more active than that of my colleagues, for I do not fancy that any of them succeeded in getting his personal actions made the subject of questions in both Houses of Parliament. Besides the particular adventure that interested Parliament I spent two years as a belligerent in the various brawls that took place in churches. This prevented my æstheticism, by that time intense, from displaying any of the effeminate characteristics associated with it in popular opinion. The lilies and languors of decadent literature were accompanied by the roses and raptures of hitting the noses of militant young Kensitites. I emphasize such behaviour because it seems important to resolve the æstheticism of the 'nineties into the component parts of reaction, romanticism, and individualism which combined to feed it. The twentieth century has brought a clarification, and it is difficult now to perceive the kinship between the cold-blooded intellectualism of Bloomsbury and Chestertonian medievalism. Yet in the 'nineties they could both have found shelter under the spreading branches of æstheticism.

In France a similar disintegration has been

perceptible. The Parnassians obeyed the spirit which had once prompted the romanticism of Victor Hugo and his followers. The Symbolists became in their turn the heirs to the Parnassian attitude, and from them emerged the French neo-Catholic group of whom Paul Claudel has reached the most genuine renown. At the same time, æstheticism in France produced its active exponents. Neo-Catholicism in literature led ultimately in one direction to Léon Daudet and the *Action Française* group, while in another direction it became associated with the nationalism of Maurice Barrès.

Another active impulse that owed much to æstheticism was social reform. Many of the best known and most effective centres of Anglo-Catholicism were associated as much in the minds of their opponents with radicalism, socialism, and all the other dread "isms" of proletarian upheaval as with religion. The old terms High Church and Low Church used by many to distinguish an Anglican place of worship where the clergyman wore a chasuble from one where he wore a black gown had by now become unsuitable. These fervid Anglo-Catholic centres had no kind of spiritual sympathy with the Toryism once upon a time associated with High Churchism. Politicians now perceived in the increasing power and influence of Anglo-Catholicism a democratic threat. A novel like

*Stephen Remarx*, published in 1893, gives a good picture of the general attitude to what were considered the revolutionaries as much as ritualists. That the author, J. G. Adderley, should have been a clergyman and the son of a peer was taken as evidence of the corrupting effects of the ritualism that good Queen Victoria and Mr. Disraeli and Mr. Punch had tried so hard to suppress. The theme of the clergyman losing his faith when confronted by the objections to faith put forward by such "great" minds as Haeckel was out of favour. Clergymen in the 'nineties had to find their "difficulties" in their efforts toward social reform. To this, of course, fleshly temptation had to be added. One of the most preposterous novels ever written appeared in 1899. That was *The Christian* by Hall Caine. Hall Caine's instinct for what would appeal to the populace was still keen; but his attempt to expound modern religious thought and behaviour was not justified by the author's knowledge of social or religious life. The caricature of Anglican religious life in *The Christian* seemed to bring the clergyman as a subject for popular fiction into discredit, and it was some years before any novel dealing with ecclesiastical subjects had the least vogue.

The medievalism of William Morris did not include religion on its road to socialism. Religion, so far as William Morris was concerned,

G

was confined to an occasional exclamation in a
poem like:

> *Pray but one prayer for me 'twixt thy closed lips,*
> *Think but one thought of me up in the stars.*

The side of medievalism that attracted Morris
was craftsmanship, and he saw no hope for the
future of the English handicraftsman unless
socialism protected him against the capitalist.
His socialism, however, had much more in common with the distributism advocated by G. K.
Chesterton than with the socialism we now
associate with politicians.

Another romantic socialist was Cunninghame
Graham, who gave to the cause the best of
knight-errantry, and who in the famous Trafalgar
Square riots of the 'eighties fought as valiantly
as one of Roland's men at Roncesvalles. But
though socialism was making its appeal to roman-
tics, whether they were medievalists like Morris,
or chivalrous aristocrats like Cunninghame
Graham, or ritualistic parsons in the slums, the
formation of the Fabian Society in 1884 had
made its appeal to middle-class prudence, and
it had gradually cornered most of the intellectual
support available. It might be as well to remind
readers that the Fabian Society took its name
from the Roman general Quintus Fabius Maxi-
mus, known as Cunctator, who upset Hannibal's
plans after the Carthaginian victory of Cannæ by

a defensive campaign of delay. The Fabians were pledged to support socialism in our time not by getting a bloody coxcomb like Mr. Cunninghame Graham in Trafalgar Square or indeed by any revolutionary action of the mildest kind, but by harassing the enemy with pamphlets and supporting the spirits of its members by debates. One of the most prominent members was Mr. Bernard Shaw, and it may be said that the present attitude of mind loosely called internationalism originated in the Fabian Society. Until that society supplied a rallying ground for intellectuals who were in favour of reform, but were opposed to violence, the kind of attitude they promoted had been almost peculiar to the Quakers.

# CHAPTER XI

## THE BOER WAR

THE outbreak of war in South Africa in 1899 brought to an abrupt end the crisis in the Church of England, swept away the decadent æstheticism which had survived the Oscar Wilde case, solidified the radical elements of the country, and finally destroyed the prestige of Victorianism for the younger generation. I am not trying to sustain a paradox when I say that everything which has been attributed to the effect of the European War 1914–18 had been already brought about in this country by the Boer War. When we consider even now the capacity of those two words "British Empire" to stir the pride of the average man it is surprising to turn back the pages of British history and find how brief was the time during which that conjunction of words possessed any extended significance. There were jingoes in the late 'seventies, but they were something entirely different from the jingoes of the 'nineties:

*We don't want to fight, but, by jingo, if we do,*
*We've got the ships, we've got the men, we've got the money too.*
*We beat the Bear before, boys, and if we're staunch and true,*
*The Russians shall not have Constantinople!*

The conception here is of the British bulldog protecting the gentlemanly Turk against the truculent Russian Bear. The pride of the country is expressed in the fancy that a little 'un like England is plucky enough and clever enough to knock out a big 'un like Russia. But there is no talk of the white man's burden or the Pax Britannica. There is no hint in literature of any comparison between the Roman Empire and the British Empire. The history of the British Empire as presented by books appeared to be the result of a series of virtuous and violent spasms by the English, in which their exceptional ability to handle ships, the favour of Almighty God extended to them and greatly increased after the Pope had been chased out, and the inevitable assistance of the weather had combined to help them to paint the greater part of the globe red. Unreasonable behaviour by Scotland, and later on even more unreasonable behaviour by Ireland, had temporarily diverted the English from that noble task of painting the world red; but there was seldom a hint of any purpose in such painting beyond the accumulation of other people's territory and trade. The idea that the British Empire was based on the truth of the proposition that if the whole world were painted red it would be a better place is nowhere expressly stated.

The first writer who deliberately set out to train statesmen in their responsibilities to the Empire was J. R. Seeley. His books, *The Expansion of England in the Eighteenth Century*, published in 1883, and *The Growth of British Policy*, published in 1895, had considerable influence in giving shape and deliberate purpose to a vague almost instinctive imperialism. Seeley's books had no popular vogue. It was left for Mr. Rudyard Kipling in the decade between the Jubilee of 1887 and the Diamond Jubilee of 1897 to put before the people of Great Britain a conception of their importance to civilization and to assure them of their successorship to Imperial Rome. The great Diamond Jubilee procession on that fine June day of 1897 seemed to offer to the country and to the rest of the world as visible a token of the miraculous power and might and glory of the British Empire as if the Albert Memorial had suddenly taken it into its head to stalk in solemn state from Kensington to Ludgate Hill, followed by the one hundred and seventy symbolical figures of virtues and sciences on the marble frieze and the four groups of zoological statuary that represented the four continents over which British rule had spread.

It is not suggested that Mr. Rudyard Kipling alone popularized imperialism. Lord Salisbury had made Alfred Austin poet laureate in 1896 soon after *The Times* had published his turgid ode in celebration of the Jameson raid. It was Kipling, however, who invented the mystical value of British imperialism; it was he who romanticized every individual who did his bit for the British Empire, from Tommy Atkins in India to the Queen-Empress herself. It was he who supplied the people of Great Britain with the notion that their desire to rule inferior races was inspired by nothing except the austere consciousness of a moral duty. By force of genius he imposed upon the public a set of figures as mythical, if by their resemblance to ordinary human nature they are to be judged, as centaurs. No colonel or subaltern or private soldier ever talked or acted like the colonels and subalterns and private soldiers in Rudyard Kipling's tales and poems; but they were accepted as authentic, and with the wider and wider circulation of his books they grew more and more impressive, so that, when in the autumn of 1899 the British Empire went to war with two obstinate little Dutch republics in South Africa, the general feeling was that a couple of street scavengers had tried to hold up the Diamond Jubilee procession. That eighteen years before one of those Dutch republics had defeated the British Empire at Majuba was remembered only as another example of Mr. Gladstone's inveterate lack of patriotism.

To Mr. Kipling's poetical expression of the British Empire's responsibility to the future of civilization there was added in 1896 a still more potent missionary force. This was the publication of the *Daily Mail*, with which for the first time the influence of the Press really began to exercise an influence over the family as distinct from father himself. There had been earlier attempts at family newspapers. The *Daily News*, founded as long ago as 1846, had been one, but they had none of them reached beyond pater-familias. The nearest approach to a really popular newspaper had been the *Daily Telegraph*, the first to be published at a penny, and in 1896 able to boast on a large placard "Over Half a Million daily. Largest Circulation in the World." In the 'eighties the *Telegraph* had seemed sensational enough. People spoke about Telegraphese when they wished to rebuke a certain kind of florid and pretentious style of writing. I do not recall that any attempt was made in the columns of the *Telegraph* to expurgate the legal reports in the interests of family morality, although their dramatic critic Mr. Clement Scott used to shriek as hysterically in defence of the home's purity when assailed by plays like Ibsen's *Ghosts* as nowadays the agonized chastity of Mr. James Douglas moans under the rack of novels like *The Well of Loneliness*.

There is a popular tradition that the *Daily Mail* succeeded because it was ruthlessly sensational and cost but a halfpenny. That the lowness of the price may have helped is certain, because it enabled the *Daily Mail* to get into many homes at first when it was still a novelty as a supplementary newspaper, but that sensationalism had much to do with its success is false. I remember as well as yesterday reading the first number of the *Daily Mail* in the street on my way back from school. I remember taking it home and announcing that I had discovered a paper which was much more interesting than the *Telegraph*, and asking if it might be taken in by us instead of the *Telegraph* when my father was away, and in addition to the *Telegraph* when he was at home. My father would not consent to relinquishing the *Telegraph* whether he was at home or not. He had been reading the *Telegraph* all his life, and he would have felt it disloyal to exclude it from our house even in his absence. However, he agreed to admit the *Daily Mail*, although to the end of his life he never read it and regarded it as to-day an old reader of the *Daily Mail* might regard the Children's Supplements on Tuesday, Thursday, and Saturday. It is worth recording that unlike the rest of the Conservative Press the *Daily Mail* treated the Anglo-Catholic party in the Church of England with fairness, indeed with sympathy. It also threw its rapidly increasing popular influence on the side of the war party in South Africa and cannot be exonerated from encouraging some of the unpleasanter external aspects of patriotism.

It was the *Daily Mail* which engaged Rudyard

Kipling to write the words and Sullivan to write the music of a song intended to stimulate the public into subscribing to a fund in aid of the wives and families of soldiers ordered to the front. This was the genesis of *The Absent-Minded Beggar*. It was a deplorable lyric, and the method of raising funds was hardly less deplorable. The hysteria of the country during that autumn of 1899 was acute, and not even the Germans in 1914 succeeded in sinking to such low depths of blatant and vulgar self-assertiveness. The early reverses of the British arms made the hysteria more intense, and the thought of the Expeditionary Force of fifty thousand men on the way to Cape Town filled the mob with bloodthirsty pride. The London populace wore Union Jack waistcoats, ties of scarlet and khaki or of navy blue and khaki, and buttons with the heads of generals on them. Songs much worse than *The Absent-Minded Beggar* were bellowed everywhere. A picture of Joseph Chamberlain thrown on the sheet at a music-hall cast the audience into a delirium.

The Expeditionary Force reached the Transvaal and proceeded to lose every battle it fought. Something seemed to have gone wrong with Mr. Rudyard Kipling's Empire, and the *Daily Mail* was not slow to say so. It is an immense pity that the criticism in which the Press of Great Britain indulged itself during the Boer War

was so successfully burked during the war of
1914–18. The impression which contemporary
chroniclers give of the state of the country
during that black January of 1900 suggests a
grave and dignified nation stiffening its back
and setting its teeth to fight for its life. Do
not believe it. The hysteria was acute. London
was filled with City Imperial Volunteers and
Imperial Yeomen, to intoxicate whom every
night was considered a glorious display of
patriotism. However, any insurgent doubt
about the reality of the Empire was calmed by
the news that the Colonies were sending volunteers to South Africa. Public hysteria reached
its height with the relief of Mafeking in 1900,
after which it mercifully subsided. The Conservative Party took advantage of the country's
mood to fight the Khaki election. The out-
rageous deficiencies which almost every government office had displayed during a war for
which they had had four years of office to pre-
pare were forgotten. The gods, pardonably
anxious to destroy the Conservative Party, drove
it mad first, and from that fatal Khaki election
of 1900 it never recovered its prestige.

It may be said that the conduct of the Boer
War turned almost every young man with the
smallest amount of brains and imagination into
an anti-Imperialist, and those who discern in
the recent votes registered at the Universities

against war a genuine spirit of peace will be wise not to place too much confidence in the endurance of such a spirit. Disgust and weariness of war were as much a feature of intellectual life at the beginning of the century as they are now. No important work of literature was begotten by the Boer War, and, although Mr. Kipling has managed to retain a good deal of the esteem of his countrymen, that war dealt his muse a mortal blow.

# CHAPTER XII

## JOURNALISM AND LITERATURE

YET the *Daily Mail* grew in power year by year. Not even the untrue publication of the massacre of the staffs of the Legations in Peking in the summer of 1900 seriously checked its progress, and the influence it exercised over popular opinion did not diminish until the journalism which it had brought into existence became characteristic of all British newspapers. The extent to which it had revolutionized the position of the Press was revealed when the *Daily Mirror* was launched as a woman's paper. The fiasco was complete. What might have been a success in 1896 was not wanted a few years later. Women were reading the *Daily Mail*. They had not the least desire for a paper of their own. The *Daily Mirror* was hastily turned into a picture paper, and with this improvisation initiated another phase of journalism.

The revolution which the *Daily Mail* effected in daily journalism had already been effected in the monthly magazine by the publication in 1891 of *The Strand Magazine*, though actually *The English Illustrated Magazine* was the first to break away from the old-fashioned traditions of such publications as *Temple Bar*, *The Cornhill*, and *Chambers' Journal* by including pictures among its stories and articles. It was probably the rapid increase in popular monthly periodicals that made the reduction of the price of the novel an imperious necessity. Hall Caine and William Heinemann were responsible for the killing of the three-volume novel, and though the reduction of prices was no doubt commercially inevitable the artistic advantages of it were doubtful. A novelist like George Meredith, for all his complaints about lack of public appreciation, was able to obtain a price for a new novel which would make a contemporary highbrow novelist sleep uneasily for a week for fear of becoming popular. The four hundred pounds advance for a Meredith novel, though it might compare unfavourably with the ten thousand pounds paid to George Eliot in the same year, represents at the present value of money an advance of at least seven hundred and fifty pounds, and a novelist like D. H. Lawrence, who was the equivalent of Meredith in standing, never received such an advance. Indeed, right through the nineteenth century novelists with large or limited publics received a much higher reward than their less fortunate successors to-day. Thackeray was paid three hundred pounds for an instalment of *Pendennis*, which ran for three years in *The Cornhill*. He must have received for the serial rights of the novel something like nine thousand pounds. Such a price was never paid in America even at the height of the boom, and no English magazine has paid anything like that for a serialization in more recent times. If the amount of money received for the fifteen hundred or so new novels that are published every year were pooled, I doubt if an average year without one of those wild best-sellers would allow a distribution of more than twenty pounds for each novel. It is true that the modern novelist has the advantage of the American and Colonial markets, but royalties in the Colonies are low, and comparatively few British authors enjoy more than a fleeting taste of American favour on any generous scale. For some time, particularly just after the war, serialization in magazines provided a rich addition to book sales; but the popular magazines have been badly hit by wireless, and also by the poaching of many of their features by the daily papers, which are forced to maintain the huge circulations with which they have embarrassed themselves. The profits from novel writing are more likely to decrease than increase in the future, and the strictly professional novelist may become extinct after the death of the few representatives left of what already seems a prehistoric monster.

With the extinction of the professional novelist we should probably see the extinction of the professional reviewer. Reviewing was in its glory during the 'nineties when there were more

London morning papers, nine or ten evening papers where there are three to-day, and a host of weekly reviews. What the *Saturday Review* or the *Athenæum* or the *Speaker* or the *World* said about a new book was of importance. Speaking from my own experience I can say that as late as 1911 a moderately favourable review of my first novel in the *Spectator* on Saturday produced an order for five hundred more copies in the libraries on the Monday morning. Even more important to the author than the amount of sales these weekly reviews influenced was their ability to confer upon a new writer a reputation. The greater part of this criticism was anonymous, though one or two reviewers like W. L. Courtney in the *Daily Telegraph* signed their reviews of the book they starred that week on the literary page they edited.

With the decline of the weekly reviews the influence of criticism became less perceptible. The habit of signed literary criticism in the daily Press grew, and with the growth of it the quality of criticism deteriorated. Plurality crept in and the effect was as bad on criticism as it had been on the Church. A man hesitated to damn a book three times over in three papers, and his praise of it after three repetitions in slightly different language sounded mechanical. Another weakness of signed criticism was the suggestion it seemed to offer of log-rolling, though actually log-rolling could be carried on with more success anonymously. Then the *Evening Standard* persuaded Arnold Bennett to take up again under his own name the admirable reviewing he had done once upon a time in *The New Age* under a pseudonym. Fantastic powers of influencing the success of a book were attributed to Bennett. It was believed he had only to praise a novel warmly in the columns of the *Evening Standard* to make it a best-seller. All that Bennett could do and, let me add, all that any critic can do is by the enthusiasm of his praise to persuade some of the public to buy a new book. Then if the public taste coincides with his own, personal recommendation will ensure the book a run.

After the success of Bennett's criticisms in the *Evening Standard*, other papers enlisted the services of well-known novelists to write about books. I suppose I may call myself a conspicuous example of the novelist-critic, and I do not believe that the system is good for criticism. My reasons, however, for such an opinion have nothing to do with the popular legend that novelist-critics spend their lives in an atmosphere of graft promoting the sales of their colleagues. My chief objection to the signed criticism of a novelist in a paper with a huge circulation is that it is his duty to find each week as many books as he can that his vast and hetero-

H

geneous body of readers will enjoy, in the course of which duty he is compelled to praise the books he praises in their own class. This gives the impression of over-praising. The impression becomes one of fulsome adulation when the publishers with the help of asterisks quote his praise as a testimonial to their wares. There is no doubt that the average novelist-critic does err on the side of kindness, for he must be anxious not to allow his personal prejudices any chance to assert themselves. The advertising demands on a newspaper's space in these days make it more and more difficult all the time to find room for many books that deserve notice. Hence, in the space at his disposal the novelist-critic is anxious to do as much as he can to help any book that deserves a measure of prominence. Those disgruntled young authors who write fierce articles in the American and Colonial Press, denouncing the corruption prevalent in contemporary literary criticism, should remember that, unless the daily papers employed men and women with names to write about books, books would not be written about at all nowadays except in an exclusive literary organ like the *Times Literary Supplement*, where a happy anonymity is still able to maintain itself and secure attention.

Those who sigh for a return to the brutal methods of the *Quarterly* and the *Edinburgh* would be the first to file an action for libel if they were the victims of such criticism, and it should be clear even to the most fanatical young Savonarola of literature that no editor of a paper with two million readers would allow even the most eminent novelist of the day to print the political abuse which a century ago so often masqueraded as literary criticism. If good literary criticism is less in evidence to-day than formerly, the blame rests with the reading public. It can be found by those who take the trouble to search for it and are willing to support the periodicals that offer it. Critics like Edmund Gosse and his successor in the *Sunday Times*, Mr. Desmond MacCarthy, have maintained a standard of cultivated opinion. Mr. Gerald Gould in the *Observer* and Mr. Ralph Straus in the *Sunday Times* have for years given fair treatment to the three or four hundred novels they have to read every year. In papers like the *Glasgow Herald* and the *Manchester Guardian* the anonymous reviewing is of the best quality. We have no Matthew Arnold or William Hazlitt, no Coleridge scattering the treasures of his mind in *Biographia Literaria*. And we certainly have no Samuel Johnson. The only consolation is that if we had them they would be no more capable of dealing with the flood of literature to-day than the critics we have.

# CHAPTER XIII

## A SUMMER'S READING IN 1900

DURING the summer of 1900 I read about one hundred and fifty novels, most of which had been published in my short lifetime. In the early spring of that year, depressed by the intolerable boredom of school, I announced my intention of getting out to the war in South Africa unless I were allowed to leave school and go abroad. My young brother, two and a half years younger than myself, had run away from school and, although not yet fifteen, had almost succeeded in enlisting in the Imperial Yeomanry, so that my chance of being accepted at seventeen seemed probable. Anyway, after a series of struggles and adventures which need not be told here, I found myself at the end of June in the heart of the Lyonnais, staying with a French uncle, the shelves of whose house were packed with lemon-yellow French novels and many volumes of the Tauchnitz editions of English novels, the jetsam of various wanderings over the Continent by American cousins.

Of early novels those of Henry Kingsley made the deepest impression. I read *The Recollections of Geoffrey Hamlyn*, *Ravenshoe*, *The Hillyars and the Burtons*, and others. At the time they conveyed a sense of spacious life, but I have never had an opportunity to re-read them, and I

have no idea how they would appeal to maturity.
I could never stand the novels of Charles Kingsley; even *Westward Ho!* was an exasperation.
Yet *The Heroes* had been one of my favourite
books in youth. I remember a fierce argument
with a novelist uncle, one of the Meredithian
victims, in which I defended Kingsley's prose
against his sneers at the softness of its pseudo-
poetical quality. I fancy that the superiority of
Henry Kingsley's novels over his brother's lay
in his greater skill in the creation and evocation
of character. Most of Charles Kingsley's people
were walking pulpits in different styles of architecture.

This would have been the time to read
Anthony Trollope, but he was only represented
on the bookshelves by *The Warden*, by which I
was suitably moved. I have never read any other
novels by Trollope, though I have always known
that I was missing something good by not doing
so. However, the more recently published books
I read that summer at Charnay were probably of
more use to my development than earlier novels
of established reputation. A preoccupation with
æstheticism while developing one side of my
taste had left it too exclusively attracted to the
bizarre and fantastic for the acquisition of a
balanced judgment. Circumstances drove me
into seeking entertainment from less exotic literature, and undoubtedly this intensive study of

the social problems of the 'nineties through the
medium of current fiction knocked off many of
the corners of the awkward age. After *Mademoi-
selle de Maupin* and *À Rebours*, after the *Méphisto-
phéla* of Catulle Mendès and Gabriele d'Annun-
zio's *Trionfo della Morte*, after the Satanism of
*Là-Bas*, the necrophily of Rollinat, the fantastic princesses of Maeterlinck, and the volup-
tuous horrors of Baudelaire's black Venus, it was
about time to be able to find Rhoda Broughton's
novels the most moving love stories I had read.

*Cometh up as a Flower*, *Not Wisely But Too
Well*, *Red as a Rose is She*, *Nancy*, *Belinda*, each
one seemed to me more exquisitely true than
the last; but they were all written in the historic
present, and the consciousness of that has prevented my attempting ever to read them again,
because I would not for the world spoil the impression they made upon me in the heart of
France thirty-three years ago. Their titles bring
back the jasmine-covered arbour in whose shade
I used to sit, and the lizard-haunted terrace that
overhung the dazzling dusty road along which
the great white cows drew their burdens and
the swallowtail butterflies tumbled in creamy
flight. A year or two later I was to meet Miss
Broughton in person in that little house at the
top of Headington Hill that was all chintz and
old silver, herself silvery-headed, with an eye as
bright and reflective as the bowl of her Georgian

teapot and a tongue whose wit was as sharply fragrant as the tea she poured from it. Miss Broughton's historic present might seem painfully dated nowadays, but I do not intend to find out. It remains in my memory alongside *Cranford* and *The Vicar of Wakefield*, and when I read those books over again I often think how much I should like to read *Red as a Rose is She* over again, but I always have the wisdom to refrain.

And then after Miss Broughton's novels came the incomparable pleasure of reading George du Maurier's *Trilby* for the first of many times. That set me off reading Murger's *Vie de Bohême*, and when I had finished that, *La Dame Aux Camélias*, which I should call a perfect experience for a boy of seventeen, especially when it was followed by *Eugenie Grandet*. Oh, to read *Eugenie Grandet* now and be able to find myself sitting paralysed with the emotion of it and unable to turn over the next page in the dread of hearing old Grandet ask his daughter for the coins in the money-box which she had given to her lover! I should like to tell of the struggle with a pious aunt on the verge of entering a sisterhood over my right to read *La Cousine Bette* and of a more worldly aunt's defence of my right to read it. But the adventures of a boy of seventeen with Balzac's novels would make a book in itself, and indeed a book has been made about it by Mr. Robert Hichens, who a couple of years later was to publish *Felix*. I have not re-read those early books of Mr. Hichens. At that time *The Londoners* seemed the funniest book I had ever read, and *Flames* the most profound and daring piece of realism it was possible to write in English. After *Flames* neither *The Woman Who Did* by Grant Allen nor *The Yellow Aster* of Rita justified for me the sensation they had caused when they first appeared.

At this period I read nine novels by Henry Seton Merriman right off the reel. I fancy that they would all bear re-reading, and I intend to make the experiment when the opportunity presents itself. Merriman did provide his readers with an illusion that they were moving intimately behind the scenes of European politics, and he shared with Rudyard Kipling an ability to present commonplace people with an apparent omniscience that deceived the reader into supposing that it was possible to generalize about a man's behaviour from his superficial characteristics. I recently read through most of Mr. Kipling's earlier short stories, and found that his tricks were still capable of bewitching one after a wide experience of the world, and I have a notion that Merriman's novels might perform the same feat for experienced maturity. It is a pity that Seton Merriman did not live long enough to give us some stories about the last war.  He was only forty when he died, and his achievement was considerable.

*Diana Tempest* and *Red Pottage* by Mary Cholmondeley remain in mind as exciting adventures in reading, but I fancy both novels would seem stilted nowadays.  A ridiculous book by Marie Corelli called *The Mighty Atom* was still able to impress me at this date, but that was the last of her novels I could read.  Can anybody read them now?  Many explanations have from time to time been put forward to explain the vogue of notorious best-sellers, but the long popularity of Marie Corelli among readers of apparent intelligence now seems beyond any hope of explanation.  Ouida could tell a good story, and even in these days if one is ready to pass with a smile over a few absurdities the best of her novels are readable.  Such an assertion is strengthened by the support of Norman Douglas, who has always been a staunch champion of one at whom it was the fashion to sneer when Marie Corelli was still being taken seriously.  To Hall Caine with all his vulgarity and bombast we can still grant a measure of respect, and the raptures of critics over his earlier books in the late 'eighties and early 'nineties may be condoned.  Nothing can be said in favour of Marie Corelli or the critics who extolled her.

Ellen Thorneycroft Fowler's epigrams might seem mechanical nowadays, but in 1900 when I read *Concerning Isabel Carnaby* and *A Double Thread* I thought that wit was incapable of a more intense brilliancy. *The Heavenly Twins* and *The Beth Book* of Sarah Grand opened a door to contemplate what was then called the New Woman. *The Silence of Dean Maitland* had been published as early as 1886, but it was still being read, and I remember to my shame enjoying it more than *The Scarlet Letter* by Nathaniel Hawthorne, the theme of which was similar. Those who, praising deeds of the past, demand from contemporary novelists more in the way of a story than they usually provide are apt to forget with what fantastic stories novelists were wont to impose upon their public. Take *The Silence of Dean Maitland*. A curate seduces a girl, commits manslaughter, and allows his best friend to undergo penal servitude for the crime. When the friend is released from prison the curate has become a dean, and on being forgiven by the unfortunate friend confesses his crime publicly in the pulpit of his cathedral, as I remember, and dies *coram populo*. This is the kind of stuff that people called a good story, and I may be forgiven for maintaining that we have advanced beyond such manufactured fustian.

On the other hand, *Ships that Pass in the Night* by Beatrice Harraden probably was a really good novel, though, to be sure, that was nearer to the plotless affairs of to-day that irritate the

story lovers. I have already alluded to *The
Prisoner of Zenda* and *The Dolly Dialogues* of
Anthony Hope, and there is no need to paint the
lily by praising *The Prisoner of Zenda*, which, in
its own genre, has never been surpassed and is
never likely to be surpassed. Yet in some ways
*The Dolly Dialogues* is a more important book,
for the technique of it, which was entirely new,
really taught modern novelists how to write
natural dialogue. I took the trouble to look into
this question rather carefully some years ago,
and it is surprising to find what an advance the
dialogue of novels made after the publication of
Anthony Hope's book. At this date I read an
early story of W. J. Locke's called *Derelicts*, as
gloomy a tale as could be imagined, remote indeed from his pleasant and sentimental unrealities
of later days. *Susannah* by Mary E. Mann is a
novel which remains vividly in my memory from
this period, and *Tales of Mean Streets* and *A
Child of the Jago* by Arthur Morrison seem in
retrospect full of the boldest realism. And I have
forgotten John Oliver Hobbes. *The Gods, Some
Mortals, and Lord Twickenham* seemed the quin-
tessence of life's knowledge, while *The School
for Saints* seemed to display as much knowledge
of the Catholic temperament as Mrs. Humphry
Ward's *Helbeck of Bannisdale* seemed to lack.
*The Gadfly* by E. L. Voynich was one of the
most exciting adventures with those books in

France, and it remained as a masterpiece in my fancy for many years, until I unfortunately came across a copy of it one day and started to read it again, only to discover that it was completely absurd.

The novel which of all others cast the deepest enchantment upon that summer was George Moore's *Evelyn Innes*, and though I feel confident that were I to re-read *Evelyn Innes* now I should still find it a great novel, I refuse to take even the faintest risk of disillusionment. I cannot afford to find that the Celtic poet who lived as I remember in a flat high up off the Euston Road was a caricature of Mr. W. B. Yeats. I cannot afford to spoil my memory of Evelyn's operatic triumphs. I cannot afford to find that the technique of that wonderful chapter, in which the progress of Evelyn's love-affair was suddenly indicated in the middle of it by the appearance of her lover in pyjamas after what seemed the most astonishingly powerful and daring lacuna in fiction, was perhaps a little cheap. I will not lose that exquisite picture of a visit to the Dulwich Gallery on a fine autumn day, nor the magical personality of Evelyn's father, nor the analysis of the part of Kundry in Wagner's *Parsifal. Evelyn Innes* provided one of those vital experiences by which one is led a step further in mental development. Life was changed after reading it, for it was the crown of that summer's intensive reading which came to an end with a long night journey from Lyons to Paris in a carriage packed with fat provincial mayors who had been invited to the Paris Exhibition.

I still recall the heavy garlic-hung air of the compartment, the windows of which had been kept closed all night after the horrified expostulations of nine provincial mayors when I tried to open one. I can still see after a sleepless night the limpid blue of the September sky above and the forest of Fontainebleau a luminous, almost an ardent green below, and the tallowy faces and black alpaca jackets of my travelling companions all a-snore in the morning light on the frowsty beige upholstery of the second-class carriage. All that day I amused myself at the Exhibition, finding everywhere hostility as a result of the Boer War and the vicious comments in the English Press on the Dreyfus case. And that night I sailed from Havre with a profound conviction that Great Britain and France must be friends again, so unbearable was it to find hostility in the France of my heart.

# CHAPTER XIV

## THE TWENTIETH CENTURY BEGINS

A JANUARY night, and a crowded theatre in north-east London. The orchestra has just played a rollicking medley of popular songs as overture of the pantomime. A silence. The curtain should be rising on the time-honoured red and green vapours of the Demon King's abode; but it does not rise. Instead it is pulled back to allow the manager to come forward:

" Ladies and gentlemen, I deeply regret to have to announce that Her Most Gracious Majesty Queen Victoria died this evening at Buckingham Palace. There will be no performance to-night."

The curtain falls back into place, and the black-and-white figure that seemed so small to be the bearer of such tremendous news disappears. There is not a murmur of conversation heard as the audience leaves the theatre. Only footsteps, footsteps.

Such were the circumstances in which a theatre crowded with Victoria's subjects heard that a reign, of which probably not a single person present could recall the beginning, was ended.

An ashen and breathless February day. The great plane trees of Hyde Park seem petrified as they rise above the dense black silent throng that hides the pale wintry grass. From the direction of Constitution Hill, with brass and cymbals and muffled drums, the Dead March in *Saul* throbs upon the air. There is no sound of music for a few moments. We catch a glimpse of plumes beyond the railings that mark the line of Park Lane, and then, as the melancholy pomp moves on toward the Marble Arch, we hear, as we shall never hear it again with such poignancy, cornets wailing Chopin's Funeral March. The procession has passed along carrying away a whole epoch with that gun-carriage on which a little old lady rides so lightly. I leave Hyde Park and walk back through the empty glades of Kensington Gardens, and as I pass the Palace I wonder what window it was through which the June sun shone on that morning when a seventeen-year-old girl was told that she was Queen.

Myself in scarlet and silver lace and white kid gloves in command of a half-company of gallant Volunteers who are preserving decorum in the narrow streets of Hertford while the herald proclaims Edward the Seventh by the Grace of God King and Emperor. And there comes back to me from that day the emotion of a new and boundless freedom, a feeling that the country has been released from what in the psychological jargon of the moment we should call an inhibition.

The consciousness of eating forbidden fruit, for all the spice it had added to literature and art in the 'nineties, had nevertheless lacked perfect health. There had always been a suggestion of surreptitious libertinage about it which had encouraged that self-conscious decadence. Now not merely had a new reign begun, but a new century had begun with it, and between the Oxford of 1901 and the Oxford of 1899 there seemed to stretch, and in my fancy still seems to stretch, a gulf even wider than that between the years before and after the Great War.

The world of to-day may be already discernible by 1899, but the perspicaciousness of H. G. Wells was still generally regarded as nothing more than clever sensationalism. We had most of us read his earlier books as we had once upon a time read those of Jules Verne. I remember some ardent youth's remarking to me enthusiastically in a school class-room in 1899 that Wells was the coming man, and I remember with what contempt I, preoccupied with æstheticism, regarded such a remark. I felt as some literary sixth-form boy of to-day might feel if a companion suggested to him that *Bulldog Drummond* or *Tarzan of the Apes* marked a new era in psychology. Fortunately for myself, during the year I was free from school and waiting to go up to Oxford, I had come into contact with various survivors of the literary tradition in which Robert Louis Stevenson, W. E. Henley, Edmund Gosse, and Charles Whibley had viewed literature. They were the kind of people who bought the Tudor Classics as they were published in preference to more exotic productions of *fin-de-siècle* literature. This meant that I began to read again the great classics, so many of which I had swallowed whole in early youth before I was able to digest them. Therefore when I went up to Oxford in the autumn of 1901, although I was buying *Yellow Books* and *Savoys*, plays by Maeterlinck, symbolist poets like Mallarmé, and binding up a complete edition of Verlaine in a special shade of green buckram that took a week to meditate over, I was also buying Montaigne and Rabelais and Cervantes in serviceable editions that did not require æsthetic bindings. I had already started on Walter Pater; but I now bought his complete works, and read and re-read them until I could quote pages by heart of *Marius the Epicurean* and all the others. What had formerly attracted by its strangeness and richness and partial incomprehensibility now attracted as an ordered system of æsthetics which seemed to offer a key to an understanding of all the arts. This period marked the peak of my devotion to Meredith, and I remember reading *The Tale of Chloe* and thinking that the human pen was

I

incapable of setting down on paper a greater eloquence of passion.

Charles Marriott's novel *The Column* had not long been published, and in that I had found confirmation of my belief that the Meredithian formula could inspire hundreds of new and marvellous novels that would revivify English fiction and destroy that sense of inferiority which the triumphs of French fiction had forced upon it. That sense of inferiority exerted a lowering influence. We were finished with the Victorian era; but Victorianism was still potent, and the prospect of any real freedom for the English novel was as yet remote enough. Hence, no doubt, the tendency to seek in the verbal elaborations of Meredith a substitute for the direct tale we could not tell in English. A writer like George Gissing had nothing to say to youth, and even to this day I cannot read him. I recognize his merit, but the temperamental antipathy to his attitude is too much for me to surmount. Meredith may have falsified life more thoroughly than Gissing, but it was the falsification our mood demanded when the twentieth century arrived. Perhaps I insist too much upon my personal attitude; but it was not a peculiar attitude, and it represents fairly what most intelligent young men at the University were thinking. Indeed, throughout those first two or three years of the twentieth century, I do not think I shall be exaggerating if I say that every new novel esteemed by youth owed its reputation to its homogeneity with the Meredithian world. My own gradual desertion of Meredith for Hardy was exceptionally early.

# CHAPTER XV

## THE OXFORD POINT OF VIEW

In my second term I became obsessed with the duty of demonstrating to the world at large that Oxford had changed its point of view completely since the 'nineties. I persuaded seven other people, most of them senior to myself, to contribute five pounds apiece to found a review that would prove this fact to the world. The first number of *The Oxford Point of View* appeared in May 1902, under the ripe editorship of myself aged nineteen and a half. A weekly paper called *The Varsity* which was founded, edited, and almost entirely written by a Pembroke man had announced in its gossip column that there were rumours of a new University magazine which was to rekindle *The Spirit Lamp*.

"We hope this is not true," he wrote. "We did not like *The Spirit Lamp*."

We, who were collaborating like so many Patagonian emus to hatch our egg, feared that it might be prematurely addled by such a rumour and we denied it with an indignation the memory of which makes me realize with what fierceness youth revolts against the immediate past. *The Varsity* need not have been perturbed. Of all the innumerable University magazines which have strutted their little hour upon the stage none ever strutted quite so solemnly and quite so dully as the first number of *The Oxford Point of View*. Yet it was received by the critics of the larger Press with a seriousness which we found most gratifying, and which we assumed, perhaps correctly, marked the interest that the rest of the country was taking in the direction along which the first young men of the twentieth century were moving. Indeed, we went so far in a preliminary announcement as to take a phrase from one of Ibsen's plays and proclaim ourselves to be those who were coming after and who were already knocking at the door. That a University review, slightly priggish, unreasonably solemn and, as it seems to me now, utterly amorphous, should sell fifteen hundred copies of its first number is an indication of the interest it aroused outside Oxford, for the support of the University itself was but a poor fraction of this.

By far the most important article we ever published was a plea by Robert Bridges for the proper pronunciation of Latin, to which we secured an answer from Robinson Ellis, the Regius Professor of Latin at the University. Bridges himself used to ferment with anxiety over the reception of his attack on the current mode of Latin pronunciation. He used to ride down almost daily on his bicycle from Boars Hill, wearing grey-striped white flannel trousers, patent leather boots, a flowered silk waistcoat, a black tail-coat, a crimson silk tie pulled through a cameo ring, and a yachting cap. He made a superb figure of a poet who had disguised himself as a man of the world in order to find out how the obscurantists of Dondom were standing his cuts and thrusts. I do not know what was the exact date when the old-fashioned pronunciation of Latin was abolished in schools; but it was certainly abolished in time for Robert Bridges to enjoy the more euphonious sounds of the modern method.

I remember that once in the middle of a tirade against the imbecility and illogicality of the old public-school Latin Primer pronunciation he picked up a volume of Herrick which was lying on my table.

"Why do you read this r-rot?" he growled with that slight stammer of his.

"Because I like him among the best of poets."

He opened the volume haphazard and read:

"Her eyes the glowworms l-lend thee,
  The shooting stars attend thee."

Then he shut the volume with a snap and tossed it to the other end of the room.

"What infernal r-rot!" he growled. "What eyes has a glowworm to lend anybody?"

Two or three years later I saw him pitch a

volume of Courthorpe's *History of English Poetry* to the other end of his room in a similar spasm of irritation.

"This man is the most abominable charlatan alive," he declared. Then he went on: "I say, have you ever heard of a fellow called Bernard Shaw? I've just been reading some p-plays by him, and they are not at all bad, you know. He's a clever fellow, I tell you. You ought to r-read him."

Legend related, I do not know with how much truth, that Bridges had never read any of Keats until he was asked to write an introduction for the edition of his poetry in the Muses' Library, after which he produced what is perhaps, and indeed I will not qualify it, what *is* the finest piece of poetic criticism in the English language. When he was made poet laureate in 1913 the popular Press discovered that he had practised medicine once upon a time and it always alluded to him as Dr. Bridges, implying by that prefix a censure of him for not responding immediately in verse to what the popular Press considered suitable occasions for the phrenzy by which the popular Press itself was so easily inflated.

Bridges was always a poet severely aloof from popularity, and yet in 1929 at the age of eighty-five, a year before his death, his long poem *The Testament of Beauty*, which was a poetic summary of progress as he had viewed it through a long life, went into fourteen editions in a year. This might seem to indicate that he had always been in advance of his time, and therefore not appreciated until his mind coincided with the mind of the new age; but I think that the sudden success of *The Testament of Beauty* was due to the appetite of the public, round about the time it appeared, for any work of literature, whether it were in prose or verse, that seemed to offer a thread of guidance through the bewildering maze into which science had plunged itself and the world. The success of *The Testament of Beauty* was of the same kind as attended Sir James Jeans's personally conducted trips round the stellar system. A world distressed by loss of faith demanded, and still demands, help from its poets and scientists. Intelligent people now read *The Testament of Beauty* and Sir Arthur Eddington's authoritative and lucid expositions of modern physical theory: others read the astrological chit-chat in the Press which debases still further a science already unjustly discredited by the charlatans it too easily encourages.

# CHAPTER XVI

## ALFRED NOYES AND JOHN MASEFIELD

THE last faint echoes of the 'nineties at Oxford were heard in a paper called *The Broad* which had a brief life in 1902, and it was in the pages of this periodical that some of the earliest verse of Alfred Noyes appeared. His first volume, *The Loom of Years*, was actually published in 1902, followed by *The Flower of Old Japan* the following year. If Alfred Noyes had been born ten years earlier or ten years later he would probably have been granted much more esteem as a poet than he has been. It is, of course, absurd to introduce "ifs" and "ans" into the genesis of a poet, but I think it will have to be admitted that the circumstances of his time do often make or mar a poet, unless he is one of those great creative geniuses who escapes from his own time and helps to mould the future.

When Noyes began to write verse he was like the gentleman in the song, "all dressed up but no place to go." Granted what was really a superabundance of melody and able to enshrine the most fugitive moment in verse the facile accomplishment of which was as remarkable in its own way as Swinburne's control of metre, he had in the first rapture of his youthful singing absolutely nothing to sing about that seemed to his contemporaries momentous. By 1902 he was too late for the mood of the previous decade, and when he prolonged it he was writing in an exhausted key. John Masefield's first volume of poems was also published in 1902, but his *Salt Water Ballads* had the advantage of an active experience of deep-sea sailing behind them. In 1908 Noyes published his epic of Drake, which, in spite of a high level of sustained narrative in verse, failed to convince the watchers over English poetry that it was anything more than an epic which Tennyson had omitted to write and which now that Tennyson was gone there was no particular reason why anybody else should write. The mood of the period had no patience with the writer who was doing all over again what had already been done; and being unable to find anything more in Noyes's great talent than the elaboration and decoration of the obvious, he was neglected by critical opinion in England and Great Britain, but received in the United States a keener and wider recognition. Even his epic of scientific discovery, *The Torch-Bearers*, which really was a most remarkable achievement, was either ignored or treated with a disdainful condescension by the intellectuals of the second decade of the twentieth century. Not that Alfred Noyes has been left without appreciation from a large circle of devoted readers in this country. Probably no modern poet except John Masefield has enjoyed a more positive evidence of approval in the size of his sales. Indeed, he had for a while a vogue with the popular Press as the poet who made poetry pay. That in itself told against him with the intellectuals. For though most of our intellectuals nowadays are typical products of democracy, they have the Englishman's dislike of anything that reminds them of a humble origin. It takes a country like Scotland, whose democracy has lasted long enough to achieve an air of aristocracy, to maintain the position of a poet like Burns against all criticism. One of the reasons for the decline of Scott's influence over his countrymen is the way in which the sentimental North Briton throughout his work has begun to obscure the Scotsman. If Alfred Noyes had been born ten years later than he was he might have been hammered by the Great War at the right age for a poet's profoundest impressions. It is true that none of the younger poets hammered by the war survived it long; but none of them ever possessed any potentiality for major poetry. Alfred Noyes did.

John Masefield worked as a journalist on the staff of the *Manchester Guardian* during the first years of the twentieth century, after his retirement from the sea, and it may have been that experience which inspired him to write

*The Everlasting Mercy*. It was not a great poem. It was not even a good poem. It possessed, however, one quality which many good poems have lacked. It was timeous. It offered what looked like clear evidence that poetry was as ready to face the facts of life as prose. And in 1911 the facing of facts was beginning to seem an ineluctable business for English literature. John Masefield in poems like *The Everlasting Mercy* and *The Widow in Bye Street* succeeded in displaying an appearance of modernity without entirely losing a measure of academic dignity.

With later poems Masefield's modernity receded, but the academic dignity was preserved and often enhanced. *Reynard the Fox* is a poem which has as much chance of life as any of the poems written during this century. His nomination to succeed Robert Bridges as poet laureate was deserved, and nobody is more likely than he to write a really great poem, which might represent to posterity this period of unusually rapid transition.

# CHAPTER XVII

## THE WAY OF ALL FLESH

THIS brief discussion of Alfred Noyes and John Masefield has taken us too far ahead. It is as well to remind readers that from 1901 to 1904 hardly one of the novelists and poets whose names are particularly associated with the first quarter of the twentieth century had published anything that profoundly influenced their immediate juniors or deeply impressed their contemporaries. It is true that half a dozen of Bernard Shaw's plays had been published; but the era of the Court Theatre had not begun, and Bernard Shaw was still regarded as a somewhat precious piece of property belonging to those exclusive circles which an intelligentsia or, as I should like to call it, a psychocracy always seeks to establish.

To be sure, Somerset Maugham's early novels had offered exciting hopes. *The Hero*, published in 1901, I recall as what seemed then a daring attack on the humbug of patriotism, of which the popular behaviour during the Boer War had given us such a nauseating dose. Maugham's popular success as a playwright a few years later, followed by the rather belated recognition of him as a novelist of high quality when he turned back to novels again, has put those earlier novels of his into the shade. I have not read them again during the last thirty years with the exception of *The Magician*, which I found poor; but my recollection of *Liza of Lambeth*, which was published when he was twenty-three, of *The Hero*, of *Mrs. Craddock*, and of *The Merry-Go-Round*, is that they were fertilizing works and vividly conspicuous among contemporary publications in fiction.

By the time of which I am writing now Hilaire Belloc's *Path to Rome* was being talked about as a hopeful sign that Belloc would fulfil in literature his undergraduate renown. G. K. Chesterton's *Twelve Types* was being lent to one's friends as the work of a man who might write something good one day. Conrad's best work was appearing, but as far as I remember was little talked of in Oxford. H. G. Wells was still regarded as a Jules Verne. Galsworthy and Bennett did not exist. We looked upon Max Beerbohm with reverence, and I remember his coming to breakfast with me in the summer term of 1904, and my inviting a most carefully chosen party of friends to share the honour of meeting the great man. Max was as shy as an inspector of schools at his first job, and we were as shy as a set of schoolgirls, so that conversation was a complete failure. Nobody, least of all Max Beerbohm himself, would claim that he has been a great force in English literature. Yet of all the figures called upon to perform the task of leaping gracefully from one period into another, none of them has managed it with such an appearance of ease as Max. None has contrived so exquisitely to make the new seem old and the old shine with newness. Of the writers in my time he is the one whose discovery I envy most to posterity.

The most important literary event of my time in Oxford was the publication in 1903 of Samuel Butler's posthumous novel *The Way of All Flesh*. I suppose if *The Way of All Flesh* had never been published at all the course of English fiction would not have run differently; but there is no doubt that the younger generation did find in *The Way of All Flesh* a point of concentration for their ideas of the Victorian age which was of inestimable benefit for putting those ideas in order. I have recently asked some of my fifteen and twenty year juniors what they think of *The Way of All Flesh*, and I gather from their replies that it has lost its effect. That is not to be wondered at. For them the minor horrors of the Victorian age have become something to laugh at or ignore. We, however, found its ruthless exposure of self-righteousness, hypocrisy, and self-deception the most tangible evidence we had that we were right in turning our backs on it and looking forward to a new world. We compared *The Way of All Flesh* with the sentimental cowardice of a book like *Pendennis*. We rose from it with a dawning suspicion that

Meredith might be a *faux bonhomme* of the intellect, whose elaborate tolerance and glittering charity might be on a level with the rest of Victorian hypocrisy. I could not pretend that *The Way of All Flesh* was generally read when it first appeared; but I know that I myself preached its wonder on all sides, and that for three or four years after I went down from Oxford more and more young people were reading it and finding it the right key to open the right door. Somewhere Bernard Shaw has paid tribute to the influence of Samuel Butler upon himself; but notwithstanding *The Way of All Flesh* it was many years before most of us took the trouble to read through the whole of that great man's works, not indeed until after the *Note Books* were published in 1912.

That *The Way of All Flesh* should have been lying in manuscript since the 'seventies amazed us. I think we felt that, if it had been published earlier, the history of our time might have been altered by its exposure of human motive. It certainly restored our confidence in the power of the English novel. It may be thought that *Tess of the D'Urbervilles* and *Jude the Obscure* should have done that already, and that the publication of the first volume of *The Dynasts* about the same time as *The Way of All Flesh*, by providing a demonstration that Thomas Hardy was in the great main channel of European culture, should have confirmed our belief in him as a novelist. Yet somehow Hardy never did seem in the main channel, and it is easy to understand why the Nobel prize was never awarded to him.

K

# CHAPTER XVIII

## QUOD SCRIBEBIS?

TOWARD the end of my time at Oxford Logan Pearsall Smith came back to the University in order to do some research work for his *Life and Letters of Sir Henry Wotton*. In the manner of his reappearance there was the suggestion of an action taken by the principal character in some exquisitely complicated story of Henry James. He was then about forty, which gave him for undergraduates the weight in counsel of Nestor himself. He was a member of a distinguished Quaker family, a product of the combined culture of Harvard and Balliol, and his ability to inspire young men with the quintessential excitement of literature has never within my experience been equalled. It is tempting to enlarge upon the variety of things we learnt from him; but his name has been introduced at this point as the expounder of a doctrine which has consciously or unconsciously influenced all the arts during the last thirty years. This doctrine was that it was no longer possible for any artist to contemplate the creation of a work of art on a large scale. The development of civilization and the increasing complication of the externals of existence brought about by the material progress of man had made it impossible to produce a whole the effect of which would not be destroyed by the multiplicity of the parts. The great simple masterpieces capable of including all humanity had been written. The modern artist, therefore, should avoid any attempt to compete with the more easily achieved ambitions of the past, and aim at producing something perfect on a small scale. It may be mentioned that Pearsall Smith himself in his own *Trivia* gave us an example of the kind of work wherein a latter-day artist might reasonably hope to succeed—brief scenes and fragmentary emotions crystallized in a sentence or two or at most a page or two of prose. He had already written many of them, and fourteen years later, after being chiselled and re-chiselled and sifted and winnowed, he was to publish in a small volume what he considered worth preserving. It may be granted at once that Pearsall Smith's counsel of perfection demanded an æsthetic ideal beyond the devotion of the average young man, and it would be an affectation to pretend that I was myself ever seriously tempted with the fancy that I could achieve it. Yet what was expressed so ruthlessly by Pearsall Smith was the doubt which existed at the back of the mind of every young man at this period. He had reached what seemed a point of saturation in the flood of past literatures which left his imagination waterlogged. We were too near the 'nineties to per-

ceive that what they had done for art was by
no means so negligible as we were beginning to
think it in the disillusionment brought about
by the conduct of the Boer War, and in con-
templating the supine pusillanimity with which
the Government had discredited Conservatism.

It is becoming a legend that the years before
the Great War offered a blessed Eden to those
who were fortunate enough to spend their early
manhood in them. My recollection of those
years finds no justification for such a legend so
far as the outlook of the artist was concerned.
The sense of freedom that the accession of
Edward the Seventh had diffused at first was
not sufficiently exhilarating to counterbalance
the deadening influence of the Party in power.
There was a material prosperity which did not
feel itself seriously threatened by the three
hundred millions the Boer War had added to
the National Debt; but it was a material prosperity that threatened artists with a prolongation
of middle-class supremacy in every walk of life.
There was no inspiration in the vision offered
by imperialists of an Empire that was apparently
to be nothing better than a grandiose extension
of the co-operative store. There was no inspiration in the doctrinaire socialism of the
Fabian Society, the end of which seemed to be
the sacrifice of individual liberty to a bureau-
cratic tyranny. There was indeed a glimmer of

hope in the first obvious steps that King Edward was taking toward the establishment of an Entente Cordiale after the many years of futile misunderstandings with France that had allowed Germany to grow strong enough to threaten Europe with a Teutonic hegemony. That any *rapprochement* with France would involve a corresponding *rapprochement* with Russia on account of the Dual Alliance was sufficiently obvious to prevent the Entente's progress beyond a sentimental exchange of courtesies into a practical political arrangement.

When in 1904 I was advocating at College debates and in the columns of *The Oxford Point of View* a formal alliance between Great Britain, France, and Russia, there was no support for the extravagant notion of an alliance with Russia; and with the coming of the Russo-Japanese War I found very few sympathizers among contemporaries with my strong pro-Russian bias.

It was about now that I began to read the novels of Dostoievsky, and in the combination of the Petrine manifestation in France, the Pauline manifestation in Britain, and the Johannine manifestation in Russia I dreamed of a perfect trinity in which for the first time Christian culture would find its full expression. Hitherto Russian literature had not influenced the intellectual life of the rest of Europe at all, widely or profoundly. The novels of Turgeniev had excited the admiration of English intellectuals,* but they had excited it as works of art, not as revelations of a different way of thinking. Turgeniev himself stood in the estimation of Russians where Henry James stood in the estimation of the Americans. He gained much more from France than he rendered back to France of Russia, and the influence he exerted upon English literature was entirely a matter of technique. It was the success of the translations of Maxim Gorki's work which first began to awaken in England a real curiosity about Russian literature. In 1901–2 six volumes of translations of his novels and short stories appeared. Of Dostoievsky only *Crime and Punishment* was at all generally known, and *The Brothers Karamazov*, his greatest novel, had to be read in a mediocre French translation until 1912. Most of Tolstoi's books had been translated, but it was some time before the grandeur of novels like *War and Peace* and *Anna Karenina* began to impress themselves upon the English imagination. The complete

---

* I apologize for using this description, but the embarrassment of English people in the presence of art has placed a veto upon the use of some simple direct word which would express less pretentiously the enjoyment of a certain standard of culture. "Highbrow" was always half facetious, and "æsthete" too quickly acquired a special and, as it developed, a contemptuous implication.

surrender of the English to the sexual taboos of
Victorian literature had associated Tolstoi in
the mind even of comparatively intelligent and
cultured people with what was considered the
scandalous sexuality of the *Kreutzer Sonata*.
*Resurrection* was more widely read, but the effect
of this was again vitiated by the unfortunate
pruriency that was still such a frequent accompaniment to English reading. Englishmen
and Englishwomen at this date really were
accustomed to divide books into pleasant and
unpleasant. When Bernard Shaw published his
*Plays Pleasant and Unpleasant* there was irony
in the title; but most of his readers accepted it
as a straightforward indication of what the plays
were about. Although it may seem scarcely
credible now, it is right to set on record that in
the 'nineties you would see the *Kreutzer Sonata*
of Tolstoi being sold with enemas and contra-
ceptives in grubby furtive little shops at the back
of the Strand.

A Russian work which made a deep impression
at this time was Merejkowski's trilogy *Christ
and Anti-Christ*, the first two volumes of which
were *The Death of the Gods* and *The Forerunner*.
By the time the translation of *Peter and Alexis*,
the final volume, appeared in 1905 that impression
had almost completely vanished and the whole
influence of Russian literature upon English
intellectuals was concentrated in Dostoievsky

and Chekhov, the latter's short stories appearing in volume after volume from 1903 onwards, completely ousting Guy de Maupassant from the dictatorship he had exercised over the short story for so many years.

Yet, in spite of the way in which English novelists were turning toward Russia and finding in that literature a refreshment and invigoration for which they had during the forty previous years only ventured to look in French literature, the mass of the English people remained obstinately suspicious of Russia, and the prospect of an open alliance which might have guaranteed the peace of Europe seemed as remote as ever.

The first positive sign that England was recovering that artistic vigour of the 'nineties, which seemed to have been extinguished by the Boer War, was the opening of the Court Theatre by J. E. Vedrenne and H. Granville Barker, and it is a useful *memento mori* to remind ourselves that if the cinematograph had been invented a few years earlier than it was, the opportunity might never have been granted to the drama to play its rightful part in the revival of artistic effort in England. This is not the place to discuss in detail the triumphs of the Court Theatre or even to pause sufficiently long to contemplate the rainbow hues of what without undue pessimism we may think of as that dying dolphin, the English stage. Yet it would be an ungracious lack of acknowledgment not to recognize that the new life so soon to become apparent in the English novel owed much to the Court Theatre. It is not suggested that without the Court Theatre the English novel would have returned to the dismal condition to which it sank during the 'eighties of the nineteenth century; but it could be maintained that the ability of the public to respond to the renaissance of the English novel was immensely helped by that concentration of intelligent opinion which the Court Theatre fostered.

# CHAPTER XIX

## JOHN GALSWORTHY, ARNOLD BENNETT, AND H. G. WELLS

THE first novel that indubitably marked the beginning of a new era was *The Man of Property* by John Galsworthy, and it was appropriate that one who was to earn fame as a dramatist through the Court Theatre should be the first to establish himself as one of the new novelists. It should be noted that Galsworthy was already thirty-nine when *The Man of Property* was published, and one may safely hazard a theory that his development as a novelist had been retarded by the unpropitious circumstances of the preceding decade. The effect of *The Man of Property* on young men handicapped like Galsworthy himself by a public-school and University education, but who in spite of this had ambitions to contribute to English literature, was electric. Coinciding, as it did, with the sweeping away of the Unionist Party by the triumphant Liberalism of the 1906 election, it seemed to express perfectly the revolt of youth against those obstinate relics of Victorianism which had retained the political power they had won by a trick at the Khaki election of 1900. In these days, when Liberalism has taken on an air of Arthurian romance and when to read the names of the Liberal Cabinet in 1906 is like reading the names of the Knights of the Round Table, it is difficult to recall how fierce and fervid and practical a creed it then seemed. That Liberal revival of 1906 had the vital quality we have learnt to associate with post-war movements in some European countries, and the absence of which after the war both in England and France may be accepted less as evidence of stability than of sclerotic age.

I remember expressing my enthusiasm of *The Man of Property* to Pearsall Smith, and I remember my dismay when he declined to recognize in *The Man of Property* the authentic note of great literature. I have to confess that on re-reading *The Man of Property* ten years ago when it was incorporated with other stories in *The Forsyte Saga*, I found a longer experience of life had left me more keenly aware of Galsworthy's faults than of his virtues. The lack of humour and, strange though it may seem to some to say so, the lack of much first-hand experience of human nature, the deliberate manipulation of the natural scene that suggested a theatrical convention, the sentimentalization of flowers and animals, the solemnity of presentation that so often verged upon something akin to pomposity, combined to destroy the edifice, which as I read took on more and more the air of one of those palaces built to enshrine the spirit of a nation at an exhibition.

The weakness of Galsworthy's method was patent when he attempted in *The White Monkey*, *The Silver Spoon*, and *Swan Song* to present a picture of England after the war. One began to suspect that his characters were lay figures dressed up with all he could learn from newspapers about the externals of contemporary manners, and in suspecting the authentic life of his later creations one began to ask if his typical late Victorians might not have been the result of a similar resolve to achieve typicality at the expense of individual life. The final verdict must rest with to-morrow, for it is only posterity that can decide whether the characters of a novelist are creatures of flesh and blood or abstractions whose life departs when the externals that once gave them an appearance of life are no longer in use. This may be a truism. Yet it is a truism which is consistently ignored by literary critics, and indeed the obvious life which some novelists have known how to breathe into their characters has often told against them with their contemporaries. Trollope was a novelist little esteemed in his day by the critics; but it is clear now that the characters in his novels enjoyed a life denied to the characters of some of his more highly esteemed contemporaries. The opinion which most intelligent young people now seem to hold of Galsworthy's work may be an anticipation of posterity's verdict; but, on the other hand, it may be the inevitable reaction which sets in against a writer immediately after his death. There is nothing more remote, nothing more incomprehensible than the immediate past. It is the fashion of five years ago that surprises us most by its incredibility, and it is much too soon yet to know whether Galsworthy's novels are museum-pieces like Pinero's plays or more temporarily dated like the fashions of five years ago.

In any case, as time goes on the reading of by-gone novels by posterity is likely to become increasingly rare. One of the most easily observed characteristics of the literature of this period is the growing lack of interest in the literature of any other period, and literary culture as we once knew it may only maintain itself at last round about the Arctic Circle where, during one half of the year, reading is a necessity. And even there the combination of radio with television will probably in the end destroy the necessity of reading during the long night.

Yet, whatever advanced critical opinion in England may think of Galsworthy's work, there is no doubt at all of his success in impressing the rest of Europe. Partly this may be accounted for by so many of Galsworthy's characters being exactly what the Continent supposes English people are. He does not surprise foreign readers with a revelation: he confirms a preconceived opinion. It has always been an Englishman's habit to despise continental judgments of his literature. That Europe should find Byron and Oscar Wilde two of the most remarkable figures in English literature during the nineteenth century confirms for the Englishman his inclination to regard as inferior beings the denizens of the rest of Europe. Insular superiority has suffered many shocks during the last twenty years, and among the younger generation there is abundant evidence of a desire to find themselves in accord with the European trend. In Legouis and Cazamian's *History of English Literature*, which is the most complete thing of its kind since Taine, the authors lay stress on the increasing cosmopolitanism of English writers, and in a footnote thirty-one contemporary writers are mentioned on whom contact with foreign countries has left a mark. Obviously this contact with Europe is likely with the development of transport to become increasingly extended, in which case Galsworthy may not retain his reputation over a long period as easily as Byron and Oscar Wilde. Yet, whatever may be the ultimate fate of Galsworthy's work, nothing can deprive him of the honour which belongs to any pioneer, and even though exclusive opinion may have perceived from the very start the weaknesses which, it must be admitted, do prevent his being proclaimed a novelist of the first class, the influence he exerted upon his immediate juniors was for a time powerful enough to make any criticism of his work by one of those juniors savour of ingratitude.

When in 1906 Galsworthy's *The Man of Property* appeared, Arnold Bennett, who was the same age as Galsworthy, had already published half a dozen novels about the Five Towns, none of which had made any deep mark; and it was not until 1908 that *The Old Wives' Tale* placed him unmistakably in the forefront of contemporary English novelists. Arnold Bennett was the self-made literary man. He was a born journalist, and with a queer mixture of cocksureness, modesty, ambition, hard work, and inquisitiveness he turned himself into a novelist of surpassing competence. He never achieved again a *tour de force* like *The Old Wives' Tale*; but he came near to doing so fifteen years later with *Riceyman Steps*. His trilogy which opened promisingly with *Clayhanger* did not sustain itself with *Hilda Lessways*, the second volume, and in the third volume *These Twain* it petered out in dullness. Arnold Bennett had not a personality that could be psychologically exploited in a semi-autobiographical accumulation of humdrum incident. His personality was better adapted to express itself frankly and simply in those pleasant little guide-books to his own career. He enjoyed his success, and to the very end he kept that enjoyment fresh, so that he never lost the pleasure of talking shop, which was what gave such a gusto to his criticism of other people's books. The permanent value of Bennett's contribution to English literature is doubtful. Like so many other products of modern life its utility is immediately obvious, but it lacks finality. There is not a single book by Bennett of which one could prophesy with confidence that it was likely to remain unique of its kind. It is easy to imagine a theme like that of *The Old Wives' Tale* being repeated and better done in the repetition. The technique he used in the *Clayhanger* trilogy of telling a story over again from another point of view has been attempted by several other novelists, and all of them seem to have found a single experiment sufficient to discourage them from repeating it. With one or two exceptions, Arnold Bennett's books succeeded in doing what they set out to do; but when one looks back at them now they appear to have set out to do very little. His enthusiasms were almost exclusively confined to the superficialities of existence. He was overmuch preoccupied by the importance of comfort and always unduly impressed by the value of material service. This may give in the future an air of complacency to his work, which the future may find as quaint as we find some of the complacency that was so predominant an emotion in the middle of the nineteenth century. Perhaps the most complete expression of Bennett himself is to be found in his book *The Card*, and *The Card* may survive when the rest of his work is forgotten. Yet we have only to compare *The Card* with *Mr. Polly* to recognize at once the superiority of Mr. Polly's author, H. G. Wells.

In recent years there has been a tendency to decry the work of H. G. Wells because he has too often substituted preaching for narrative; but if anything can be positively asserted so soon of a living writer it can be positively asserted that H. G. Wells has had a more profound and a more extensive influence upon English life and upon English literature than any other writer of the twentieth century. Allusion has already been made to the fantasies with each succeeding one of which he established a little more firmly his claim to serious consideration as one of the great imaginative minds of the epoch. When *The Man of Property* was published in 1906 Wells, who was hardly a year older than Galsworthy, had already published twenty-two books, among which were masterpieces of pure novel-writing like *Love and Mr. Lewisham* and *Kipps*. Either of them may be read to-day without the reader

L

being aware that over a quarter of a century has passed since they were first published. Both enshrine something which belongs unmistakably to our period, but which partakes unmistakably of the eternal. Neither book when it appeared roused the sensation of novelty that was roused by *The Man of Property*. Yet both possess that life against which time should not prevail.

In 1908 *Tono Bungay* was published serially in *The English Review*, and it seems strange that all those who read the first two instalments did not immediately realize that here was something of much greater importance than either *The Man of Property* or *The Old Wives' Tale*. *Tono Bungay* did not sustain itself as a work of art. It is open to the harshest criticism. Yet when the other day I re-read it immediately on top of *The Country House* of Galsworthy and *The Old Wives' Tale*, I realized that my instinctive judgment of these three books at twenty-five was supported by the experience of fifty. There is nothing in the whole of Galsworthy or in the whole of Arnold Bennett which contains such a serene assurance of perpetual life as that house-keeper's room in *Tono Bungay*.

*Ann Veronica*, published in 1909, probably played a part in moulding contemporary womanhood, which was then in the throes of the

Suffragist movement; but it is more of a social document than a crystallization of life. In 1910 *Mr. Polly* appeared, appropriately enough published in an experimental series of novels issued by Nelsons at two shillings. I say appropriately, because *Mr. Polly* deserves to last for ever as the type of the poor man who loved great literature and who, inspired by the mere sound of words, set out in middle age to seek adventure. The experiment of publishing novels at two shillings with the outward appearance of the six-shilling novels was an economic failure. As usual the only people who benefited by the lowered price were the circulating libraries. At such a price not even a masterpiece like *Mr. Polly* could establish itself as a profitable undertaking.

*Mr. Polly* was succeeded by *The New Machiavelli*, a piece of polemical pamphleteering which one of the oldest and best firms of English publishers was afraid to issue after they had set it up in type. It was not a good book, and it marked a definite limit to H. G. Wells's imaginative control of his subject. Nowadays it seems even less of a good book than it seemed at the time. Other novels like *Marriage* and *The Passionate Friends* continued to display the author less as a pure novelist than as a preacher.

In 1916 with *Mr. Britling Sees It Through* Wells published the only novel which has authentically preserved the atmosphere in England during the Great War. To read it now may seem like a nightmare, but when posterity wishes to find out how the English thought and behaved at home during the first three years of the war the only book from which they will learn will be *Mr. Britling Sees It Through*. It was not until *Mr. Britling Sees It Through* that the readers of the United States accepted Wells as a really great novelist, and it is perhaps a reflection upon Arnold Bennett's position that he should have for nearly ten years counted for so much more than Wells in the United States. I remember an American publisher's telling me in 1912 that they could not put Wells across at a time when any novel by Arnold Bennett was a best-seller. I am not one of those who sympathize with H. G. Wells's dreams of the future, and I disagree almost entirely with his view of the past. Therefore, while I can admire his *Outline of History* as an astonishing feat, I regard it as one of the most pernicious books which has been let loose upon the world. However, that does not blind me to the immense influence it has wielded over the half-baked, and until somebody can come along and beat Mr. H. G. Wells on his own ground his *Outline of History* will continue to exert what I believe to be its pernicious influence.

What I admire about Wells is his magnificent refusal to compromise with his ideas and his profound indifference to opinion. He is the only personality thrown up by modern English democracy who suggests the grand style. Arnold Bennett always seemed to me to be in literature very much what Mr. J. H. Thomas is in politics, and Mr. J. H. Thomas would not be called a democrat in the grand style. In the third volume of his *Diaries* Arnold Bennett recorded that there were very few really A 1 people at the funeral of Mrs. Wells. "Which shows," Bennett goes on, "how Wells kept out of the 'great world' and how the great world is not practically interested in Wells." One fancies a note of regret that H. G. Wells should have bothered his head so little about the "great world." Throughout Arnold Bennett's writing there is an attitude that finds its most lamentable expression in the behaviour of some Scotsmen who make good outside Scotland. It is the clever fellow from the provinces out to show these chaps in London what's what, and in return for their appreciation of him he is willing to assimilate the externals of their civilization, content to humour them, once he has proved that they cannot do without him. Wells, on the other hand, regards London as merely another aspect of provincialism, and from one end to the other of his great volume of work there is not a hint of being aware of material success as the chief object of man. This is not to say that for some readers he does not seem to attach undue importance to the superficialities of comfort. His outlook is essentially urban, and when as in *Marriage* he takes his characters out to Labrador to solve their ethical problem, Labrador becomes temporarily a suburb.

Nothing is easier than to find fault with the details of H. G. Wells's work. As a novelist he can be censured for subordinating the creation of character to the broadcasting of Wellsian ideas. As an historian he can be censured for the misleading interpretation he places upon facts, and for taking as many liberties with the figures of history as with the figures in his own novels. As a doctrinaire he can often be derided for rushing in to plant his soap-box where the very angels tread warily. Yet when his critics have stripped him of every claim to renown there remains instead of the plucked sparrow to which most men would have been reduced by such destructive criticism, a vital and significant force, the equal of which would be hard to find in modern letters. It is possible, indeed it is probable, that very little of what H. G. Wells has written will endure as English literature; but he will surely remain a mine from which the curiosity of social historians will always be excavating. And of all living writers in English he is the one whose non-existence is least imaginable when we survey the present state of English literature.

# CHAPTER XX

## JOSEPH CONRAD

IT is never easy to fit English writers into movements or groups, for no sooner do we perceive some hint of a common ground on which a classification may be based than individuality asserts itself with divergences so rapid and so abrupt that the attempted classification has to be so much modified as to make the attempt at it a waste of ingenuity. It might be true, however, I think to call Galsworthy, Bennett, and H. G. Wells democratic writers in the sense that without an extreme susceptibility to the growing force of modern democracy their background would lack the substance that gives them a measure of confidence in the value of their work.

When we turn to contemplate Joseph Conrad we find ourselves safely removed from any possibility of successful grouping and pleasurably certain that we are in the presence of an isolated artist. It is true that the influence of Conrad's manner over various young writers was perceptible enough for some years to suggest that he was founding a school. That school never materialized, because it soon became clear that Conrad's method suited himself alone and that the application of it to the general technique of novel-writing was impossible.

All progress in the novel has been effected by

the dissatisfaction which prompted the experiments of innovators who had begun to question what was seeming the too easy assumptions of their predecessors. Even as early as Fielding the sermonettes at the beginning of every chapter of *Tom Jones* indicate a kind of self-consciousness brought about by the writer's questioning his own omniscience. Not a small part of the perfection of Jane Austen's novels is due to her exquisite avoidance of abusing the privilege of omniscience. For instance, no novel by Jane Austen contains a scene in which men take part without the presence of a woman. Jane Austen never risks a reader's asking how she knew something because in her revelation of that knowledge she had betrayed a fundamental ignorance. Dickens and Thackeray obtruded the personality of the author between the reader and the story, but that very obtrusion was a clumsy attempt to justify their right to be telling a story. Meredith's self-consciousness worked itself off in verbal elaboration, Hardy's in a preposterous arrangement of circumstances. It was Flaubert who achieved the most serviceable technique by limiting life as in *Madame Bovary* to the potential purview of a single character. Henry James after devoting himself at first to the Flaubertian method gradually achieved his own involved method of narrating a story indirectly. *What Maisie Knew* leaves the reader to discover for himself the progress of an amorous intrigue as it stirs with disquiet the partially awakened mind of a little girl. Henry James became more and more labyrinthine in his technique. When H. G. Wells once described his novels as like an elephant picking up crumbs with its trunk, James was greatly hurt; but there is no doubt that at the end of his life he had himself come to very much the same conclusion about his novels, and it is significant that in a letter to his agent, J. B. Pinker, written in 1914, which was not published in his collected letters, he stated positively that he considered H. G. Wells the best of the novelists then approaching seniority, and the junior novelist whom in the same letter he picked out as the best of his age was one whose method was as far removed from Henry James's own method as that of H. G. Wells. Once when discussing with me my own novel *Carnival*, which was an attempt at the Flaubertian method of never allowing the chief character off the page, James said he doubted whether the figure of a ballet girl was substantial enough to sustain so much centralization, and in that criticism he put his finger on the weak spot of Flaubert's method, not for Flaubert himself, who never strained it by extending it indefinitely, but for novelists of less skill.

The contribution of Conrad to the technique of the novel was his invention of narrating a story by means of two or three people who had had an opportunity of knowing the facts. This method became tiresome even in the hands of Conrad himself; in the hands of his imitators it became exasperating. Nor was there any real gain for actuality. The strain of a writer's apparent omniscience upon his reader's credulity is certainly great when readers begin to question his Olympian status; but the method which offered the reader an explanation of how the writer came to know certain facts about people in his tale imposed an equal strain, for the reader could not help asking how any listener could have had the physical endurance to remain silent while such a figure as Marlow prosed on for hours, that unending and remorseless old man of the sea, as Henry James called him once to myself. The reason why Conrad adopted this device was probably less out of any desire to improve the technique of the novel than out of an anxiety to conceal his own inability to write English dialogue. Conrad was for ever proclaiming his hatred of dialogue in a novel, and in conversation he was himself always dependent on French, which should have made his disciples suspect the disinterestedness of his criticism of English dialogue.

The miracle of an Ukrainian Pole educated at Cracow beginning to learn English on a sailing-ship at the age of twenty-one, of leaving the sea sixteen years later as a certificated master-mariner, and of gradually winning for himself a place of renown in English literature is so startling that criticism has been staggered out of its calm. Not a little of Conrad's merit as a novelist is due to the means he took to surmount the handicap of writing in an acquired language. Paradoxically, the difficulty of finding the right word secured him a vocabulary larger than that of most contemporary English novelists, and this wide vocabulary gave his prose a richness which made it seem better prose than it really was.

Yet many of the felicities depended on sight rather than on sound. No writer of prose loses more than Conrad by being read aloud. His best pages are apt to sound costive and even stilted under that test. Some of the admiration he earned for subtlety and profundity was earned for him by the care with which his own difficulties with the English language made him approach even the simplest statement. The magic with which he could touch the world of his imagination partook of the magic that distance lends, and such remoteness was sometimes a false remoteness caused by the interposition between himself and his readers of a kind of gauze woven to hide his own embarrassment. His strangeness too was perhaps less the strangeness inherent in him as a foreigner than the

strangeness suggested by his own unfamiliarity
with the language in which he was writing.

It may be argued that, whatever the cause,
the effect was enviable enough, and that is true;
but what Conrad achieved by overcoming difficulties peculiar to himself provided a dangerous
model for imitators. They deliberately assumed
what he could not avoid, and many of the Conrad school of novelists suggested artificial sun-
burn or resembled those people who cover their
luggage with exotic hotel labels to supply themselves with a false nimbus of romance.

It is perhaps not a fair charge to level against
Conrad that his tales of the sea can only be read
by landsmen; but it does suggest ground for
criticism, and that this should be so does suggest
a doubt of the permanence of his reputation.
In asserting that his tales cannot be read by his
fellow-seamen I should except *The Nigger of the
Narcissus*, and it is significant that *The Nigger of
the Narcissus* was one of his earliest books,
written before he had settled down to become
something of a "literary gent." It may not be
equally significant, because it is the expression
of a merely personal opinion, when I say that of
all Conrad's books, that which in retrospect
comes back to me most vividly is *The Secret
Agent*, for that is one of the few books in which
the sea plays no part. *Lord Jim*, to which I
suppose most people would give the palm, has

always seemed to me a great short story ruined by protracted spasms of wearisome psychology.

My prejudice may be due to a surfeit of critical eulogy which was not inspired by a genuine appreciation of Conrad, but prompted by a belief that to praise Conrad reflected the critic's own good taste. Conrad always appealed to that English delight in the art which does not conceal itself. Anybody could see that he was writing, just as anybody a few years earlier had been able to see that Meredith was writing. Conrad and Meredith resembled the strong man whose veins stand out like knotted cords when he lifts the giant bar-bell. Possibly, too, I am prejudiced by the enthusiasm which Conrad roused in the United States, for, although there is a legend that several English authors of renown have found appreciation in America before they have found it in their own country, I believe that a calm examination of the facts will reveal that most of the authors thus honoured first in America did not retain their reputations with posterity. Probably the Germans are the most readily deceived by the *faux bon* in literature; but after the Germans the Americans are the most gullible.

# CHAPTER XXI

## GREAT INDIVIDUALS

I PRESUME that George Santayana's knowledge of English was not acquired in earliest youth, and in that case his command of English prose offers at least a comparable miracle to Conrad's, because Santayana really does write English prose of the first quality. The prose of philosophers has grown worse and worse during the last fifty years, and the reading of George Santayana or Bertrand Russell confers a right to ask with some indignation why such an atrocious jargon should be tolerated from other philosophers. The debasement of the English language by psychologists during the last twenty years, coinciding as it has with the abandonment of Greek and a supposed utilitarian method of teaching Latin, has been one of the corrupting causes of the present state of deliquescence in which English prose is wallowing.

If Bertrand Russell can preserve his exquisite lucidity and yet rarely write a sentence untouched by that indefinable magic of genuine English prose, it should not be counted as a superfluous labour of Hercules for other philosophers to imprison their surging thoughts in crystal. And if a Spaniard like George Santayana can demonstrate his most subtle theories of the human mind with such beauty of limpid

English we may demand at least an attempt at clarity from the rest. Perhaps Spanish gives a mastery over English that no other modern language gives. If that be the case, our investments in the Argentine may yet save English prose from complete extinction.

If I were asked what I considered absolutely the best English prose written in my time, I should reply without hesitation that it was written by W. H. Hudson. Now W. H. Hudson like Santayana must have learnt Spanish before he learnt English, and after the remark above about American literary taste it is meet to recall that W. H. Hudson was born of American parents in the Argentine. I find on looking through the dates of his published works that *The Purple Land* appeared as long ago as 1885, and I wish I could read some of the contemporary reviews of it. Balzac once asked Théophile Gautier how he contrived to write so beautifully, to which Gautier replied that he tossed his sentences into the air and that like kittens they fell upon their feet. It is difficult to imagine the sombre figure of W. H. Hudson tossing anything into the air except a wild bird he had released, and as I write that I discover the simile for his sentences. Yes, they are like wild birds released. One may sit for hours trying to analyse the way in which Hudson obtained his effects; but the secret will remain his own.

A mystery as elusive of solution as the rhythm of Hudson's prose is why his friends chose Epstein to carve his memorial in stone. The only occasion on which I doubted the infallibility of Mr. Cunninghame Graham was when he was discovered to be one of the conspirators who helped to set up Rima in Kensington Gardens. It was easy to perceive the difficulties of commemorating Hudson with a drinking-place for the birds that would not suggest a Christmas annual; but was there nothing between naturalistic sentimentality and that ghastly female pterodactyl who represents the Rima of *Green Mansions*?

The extraordinary thing about Hudson was that after leaving the Argentine in 1869 when he was twenty-eight, and coming to live a lonely and impoverished life for many years in England, he was able to write of the English countryside as intimately as Thomas Hardy and as simply as Gilbert White. No writer of prose casts one into such a despair of one's own clumsiness. About 1909 I had the good fortune to meet him in West Cornwall just after he had heard the tale of the Lelant ferryman's young seal. This young seal had been in the habit of following the ferry-boat backwards and forwards where the Hayle river swells out across a sandy bar to the Atlantic. One day the ferryman, who with his slanting eyebrows was himself not unlike a

M

seal, called the attention of one of the passengers to the young creature. Before he could be stopped this sportsman had raised his gun and shot the seal dead. The incident is related in Hudson's book about wild life at Land's End, and my memory of him is of a swarthy man sitting among the marram grass brooding on that outrage against nature.

Mr. Cunninghame Graham was mentioned above, and there is another whose English prose must have taken on an added quality from Spanish. Cunninghame Graham, with the facile terminology of what I may call the "ismatic" present, is dubbed romantic, which when trans lated means in his case that he has taken the trouble to write as well as he could about the life of a man with an appetite for living. It is typical of him that he should not possess a copy of his best book, *Mogreb-el-Acksa*, which is disgracefully out of print, although it is one of the best travellers' tales of our time, and that time is not too rich in travellers' tales of the finest quality.

The outstanding contribution to this literature is *Travels in Arabia Deserta* by C. M. Doughty, and inasmuch as the travels themselves were undertaken in the 'seventies, the publication of these two great volumes in 1888 must be regarded as only a partial triumph for the epoch with which we are occupied. Doughty, in addition to possessing the courage and endurance to carry through his mighty feat, had a theory about English prose which he put into practice during the ten years he spent in writing his *Travels in Arabia Deserta*, and those who are now trying to evolve a new verbal coinage in English that will displace the currency of words and phrases so trite with usage as to have become meaningless and no longer fit to serve as a medium for the exchange of thought might study with advantage the deliberate archaism of Doughty's style. It may be granted that the experience he was attempting to communicate to his readers was itself a recession into the past that justified his digging up a treasure of lost words which when put back into circulation were as fresh and serviceable as if minted by himself. Further, it must be admitted that what Doughty successfully achieved in prose he failed to achieve in verse, for although I believe that his epic *The Dawn in Britain* is the greatest poem this century has seen both in the attempt and in the achievement, I am aware that such a belief could only be shared by those who reached it by the same process of miraculous revelation as myself.

English, which except Greek is the grandest and richest and most expressive language used by humanity, has been undermined by a puritanism that by fostering bibliolatry gradually incul-

cated in the English mind a notion that the
language of the Bible was a thing apart from
ordinary life, the use of which except under
conditions of a specially staged emotional recep-
tivity savoured of irreverence. In fact, mumbo
jumbo set in, and when with that diffusion of
superficial knowledge which is at present known
as education the mumbo jumbo aspect ceased to
awe, what would have once seemed an irrever-
ent trespass upon the preserves of Jehovah's
chosen language came to seem a deliberate affectation, or worse still a pretentious abracadabra.
Besides damaging the English language by im-
poverishing the common speech and isolating
the Bible in a kind of lingual sanctuary of its
own, the puritans by their hostility to all art
succeeded in creating that fatal bisection of the
language into poetical and non-poetical words.
Then came the long Latin domination of the
eighteenth century, the polite influence of which
lingers in what has now become the suburbanity
of calling a napkin a serviette or nakedness
nudity.

The only other traveller of our time who can
be compared with Doughty in the ability he has
to communicate the quality of his experience by
a deliberate use of language is Norman Douglas.
Compare a book like *Old Calabria* with that
over-praised piece of impressionism by George
Gissing called *By the Ionian Sea*. As I write

that sentence I remember Lafcadio Hearn, but in retrospect his books appear like beautiful jelly-fish or sea anemones, and it is that spinelessness which makes me suspect their claim to be called great literature. Like the books of Pierre Loti, they beguile with colours the dreams of youth or inexperience, but as life continues they take on a softness that ultimately turns to a sickliness. I am haunted by a picture in one of the books of Lafcadio Hearn of the author in Japanese dress as I am haunted by a picture of Pierre Loti as I saw him in real life during the war, a corseted little French naval officer heavily rouged and powdered, an unduly old man of sixty-seven with a horrible simulacrum of youth.

The books of Norman Douglas have made a particular appeal to young men, but it is pleasant to be able to assure those young men that their fascination will not fade with experience. They will weather like the verse of Horace. I fancy that the secret of Norman Douglas's attraction for modern youth is the assurance he provides them of life's richness. The rapid shrinking of the world during this century has already sapped the vitality and curiosity of young men, and from Norman Douglas they have learned that the world is still a very much larger place than a few mechanical inventions have been making it appear. No living writer is so capable of stimulating an enjoyment of human nature, and no living writer has such a power of conjuring from the natural scene the *genius loci*. When I first met him he was engaged in sub-editing *The English Review*, which was then being edited by Austin Harrison. We are easily moved by the sight of a dejected lion in a travelling circus; but Norman Douglas offered the far more depressing sight of a satyr who had been dressed up in conventional attire and set to work in a London office. Fortunately he escaped.

By the time that Douglas was sub-editing *The English Review* it had ceased to be what it was when it started under the editorship of Ford Madox Hueffer. What is the cause of the mysterious degeneration which affects so easily a periodical? Why should *The English Review*, which two or three years earlier had been the most important periodical in England, have sunk as rapidly to the bottom of mediocrity? Good material, of which there was enough and to spare in 1908 and 1909, was by 1911 and 1912 apparently impossible to find. Yet, there were more signs in 1911 of a literary revival than there had been three years earlier under Ford Madox Hueffer, or Ford Madox Ford as he elects to be called now. *The English Review* drew into its pages every month the vitality of English letters in much the same way as *The Yellow Book* had drawn it when it started, and the part played by Ford Madox Ford in what might be

called the concentration of the English literary
forces toward the end of the first decade of this
century was invaluable. *The English Review* succeeded in achieving what after the war *The
London Mercury* attempted to achieve but never
came near achieving.

When I consider the critical minds with
which I have come into contact I find that I
have no hesitation in declaring that of the many
judgments I have listened to on literature the
least fallible of all were Ford Madox Ford's, and
I can think of no more suitable name than his
with which to bring the first decade of this
century to a close, for I do not believe that any
man was so well aware as he of the transformation that literature was undergoing, a transformation which would have taken place whether
there had been a Great European War or not,
that transformation being caused not by the
mental, physical, or moral upheaval effected by
the war, but coming as an inevitable result of
the change in human life brought about by the
increasing power of machinery, and its concomitant the rapid development of a megalo-
politan culture.

# CHAPTER XXII

THE YEARS BEFORE THE WAR

So far my task has been comparatively easy.
To be sure, bias has not been absent, nor that
prejudice which comes from having enjoyed a
book once upon a time and attempting now to
judge it by later standards which are not necessarily better standards. If to-day I may consider
that the merit of Dostoievsky as a novelist has
been much exaggerated, I cannot forget that
there was a time when each new book of his that
was translated seemed to lead me an immense
way further toward a knowledge of human
nature. It demands a complacency of which I
am incapable to be certain that growing out of
an admiration for a novelist like Dostoievsky is
not the result of the mind's having been dulled
by experience instead of having been sharpened
by it as one would prefer to suppose. I find it
impossible not to sympathize with the young
people who are fascinated by the communistic
experiment in Russia, because I can remember
so vividly my own belief of twenty years ago,
that in reading Dostoievsky I was reading
one of the forerunners of the third period
of Christian development; and although communism in its present stage may be the nega-
tion of Christianity, I often wonder whether
like one of Dostoievsky's infernal visions it

may not in the end lead to a supernal revelation.

At any rate, the influence of Dostoievsky upon myself and my contemporaries was profound during the years before the war. To the critic who pointed out that there was no evidence of such influence in our published work I would reply that the evidence will be found in an anxiety to tell the truth; and that is where my task becomes difficult, because from the moment it has been declared that the telling of the truth was the reason for writing, any judgment passed upon a contemporary writer becomes by implication an impugnment if not of his willingness to speak the truth, at least of his ability to do so. Apart from that, the business of trying to present one's contemporaries in a fair light is embarrassing. Writers like Hugh Walpole, J. D. Beresford, Gilbert Cannan, Francis Brett Young, Frank Swinnerton, W. L. George, myself, and several others had the same general idea of our direction, but our approaches were so different that each was inclined to fancy that his own road was the best road to our destination. We were lucky in having two or three years before the Great European War overwhelmed us in which to work and establish the beginning of a reputation; but some of us were unlucky in having their schemes for future work smashed up by that war. Hugh Walpole, for instance, was setting out on the assumption that the Boer War marked the division between past and present. I myself had designed *Sinister Street* to be one of two preludes to a complete survey of contemporary society in which the personages of a large and complicated series of books were to be shown in youth. The war came, and if I had continued with my scheme the war would have had to appear in every successive volume. The edifice must have crashed with the foundations I had prepared to sustain it. I fancy I am right in supposing that others beside Hugh Walpole and myself had planned schemes they were compelled to abandon.

One of the results of the comparatively late age at which Conrad, Wells, Galsworthy, and Bennett began to produce their most important work was to make the line of demarcation between them and their juniors less clear than it would otherwise have been. Conrad was fifty-three when with the publication of *Chance* his virtues as a novelist succeeded in reaching beyond a limited circle of readers. Wells had established his name as a writer of fantasies; but it was not until the publication of *Kipps*, when he was close on forty, that his potential dimension became generally apparent. Galsworthy and Bennett might be called unknown novelists during their thirties. Rudyard Kipling, who was hardly a couple of years older than

Wells, Galsworthy, and Bennett, and actually eight years younger than Conrad, seemed to belong to the previous era.

If the group of novelists who were the next to catch the attention of the critics and the public had waited as long to mature they would all have had the war well behind them before they had begun to produce work of any significance. How far the war spoiled the promise of novelists who had already made their mark between 1910 and 1914 is a question which cannot be decided until they are all dead and have completed their work.

It may have been the influence of the Russians, it may have been the reaction against the deliberately contrived tale, it may have been a sudden awareness that the development of external circumstances was forcing the novelist to extend his scope, or it may have been simply Plato's something in the air which produced almost simultaneously right across Europe a kind of novel which was beginning to be absolutely different from any kind of novel that had preceded it. Romain Rolland in France had just produced the eight or nine volumes of *Jean Christophe*, and Marcel Proust in 1911 had just published the first volume of that huge work *À La Recherche du Temps Perdu*. I remember Edmund Gosse's telling me he had just read a French novel that seemed to him an example of the same kind of impulse which had led me into writing *Sinister Street*, and Charles Scott-Moncrieff told me later that while he was translating Proust's earlier volumes he always read *Sinister Street* to achieve an English rhythm with which he could break up Proust's sentences. What vandalism, the Proustian *dévote* will exclaim. Perhaps it was, but let him try to reproduce in English those exquisite involutions without altering the original architecture of the French. Some of those parentheses would have made even Henry James gasp.

In England Arnold Bennett, J. D. Beresford, Oliver Onions, and others were setting out on trilogies. Galsworthy, though he probably had no such intention when he wrote *The Man of Property*, was to carry on the history of the Forsytes in later volumes so that at last " The Man of Property" was to occupy hardly a quarter of that great tome called *The Forsyte Saga*. Novelists who had no conception that novels which they had published last year were the first volumes of trilogies began to announce successive volumes that would turn work already published into the first volume of a trilogy.

Yet in spite of the beginnings of a new point of view about literary expression, and in spite of the obvious resolve of the new novelists to get as near telling the truth about human nature as prudish opinion would allow them, all the novelists who established themselves before the war were still too much imbued with the world of their youth to claim the modernity that has been seized by the post-war successors. They could still be condemned by the old-fashioned critic for that formlessness which was caused by their attempt to find a new form without abandoning traditional material.

The new novelists in whom a definite defiance was most obvious were E. M. Forster and D. H. Lawrence. A novel like *Howard's End*, which preserved traditional form better than many less fundamentally revolutionary contemporaries, did reveal a new sort of mind that, while unmistakably masculine, was at the same time curiously feminine. The achievement of a partially masculine point of view by so many women writers seemed likely to be accompanied by a parallel feminization of many male writers.

Even with Lawrence's first book *The White Peacock* it was obvious that a completely original writer had arisen, and in that book too there was definite evidence of feminization. Henry James himself had this feminine streak, and it may have been partly that in Lawrence which made him turn in evident revulsion from the prospect of nominating him as one of the hopes of English fiction; but only partly.

James objected to Lawrence's work because he shrank from anything that treated seriously a social life outside the rarefied atmosphere in which James liked to think that every man and woman dwelt, about whom it was worth while to write.

Early in 1914 the *Times Literary Supplement* published two articles by Henry James in which he surveyed the state of the English novel. The choice of Conrad, Wells, Galsworthy and Bennett as representatives of the present age was obvious enough. It was when he nominated his candidates for the succeeding age that the heartburning began. I have always thought that altogether too much attention was paid to his criticism, which if carefully analysed reveals nothing more than a suspended judgment. Of the four young writers he selected for special criticism, Gilbert Cannan is no longer writing, D. H. Lawrence is dead, Hugh Walpole has established himself as a fertile and greatly esteemed story-teller, and of the fourth it is not for me to speak. There were many other writers of the same age about whom he might have written with equal hope; but it happened that the four he chose were the four who illustrated most conveniently for himself the theme he was elaborating.

D. H. Lawrence never recovered from what he fancied was Henry James's opinion of him, and not all the appreciation he received from critics in every country ever succeeded in making him forget the slighting of his genius by Henry James. We may agree now that James did not recognize the full significance of a book like *Sons and Lovers*; but the explanation was always to be sought not in the failure of his literary taste, but in a temperamental antipathy to Lawrence's attitude. My own admiration for E. M. Forster as a writer is unbounded; but a temperamental antipathy to his view of life prevents the least enjoyment of him, and after a certain age admiration without enjoyment is liable to find it difficult to communicate itself. Moreover, it is possible that the ultimate verdict upon Lawrence's novels will be a hostile one, and it is too soon to declare Henry James a dullard for not hailing him more confidently in 1914. I find it difficult to believe that a book like *Sons and Lovers* will lose its life; but nevertheless I feel much more confident that the future will honour Lawrence as a poet and a writer of short stories.

Lawrence's future renown will have to fight against the handicap his declared admirers are imposing upon him. At present he is the victim of a foolish cult.

Being inwardly consumed and tormented, he never clarified his outlook. Lawrence had neither poise nor reserve. Nor had he a trace of humour. He had courage. He knew what would be the consequence if a notorious book of his should ever be published: a howl of execration. He went ahead. I think the writings of Lawrence have done good; his influence was needed by a large class of our fellow-creatures. He has done good negatively, as a warning to thinkers and on occasion to writers; positively, because his work is in the nature of a beneficent, tabu-shattering bomb. An American friend tells me that Lawrence's romances have been of incalculable service to genteel society out there. The same applies to genteel society in England. Scholars and men of the world will not find much inspiration in these novels. Lawrence opened a little window for the bourgeoisie. That is his life work.

These words written by Norman Douglas* should be heeded by those who are trying to place Lawrence where he cannot stand. It is time for those who breathed in his air to make an attempt to explain coherently what Lawrence was after. They have exalted his ethics above his æsthetics. We want to know what those ethics were. The important fact that Lawrence hammered an entirely new beauty out of the English language has been lost sight of in an effort to extract from his hotch-potch philosophy compounded of undigested early Greek theories and medieval heresies a practical gospel for to-day.

Lawrence himself succumbed to this Messianic

* *Looking Back: An Autobiographical Excursion*, by Norman Douglas. Published by Messrs. Chatto and Windus.

atmosphere with which a number of foolish
people, mostly women, surrounded him, and he
developed what our friend Max Nordau would
have called megalomania. His anti-Christian
obsession was really based on a personal jealousy
of Our Lord Jesus Christ. This may sound
extreme; but it is related of Byron that he
was jealous of Shakespeare, and the limits of
egocentricity, once it be completely surrendered
to, may lie anywhere. As early as 1919 when
walking with me along the Via Tragara in Capri,
Lawrence stopped and proclaimed twice:

"There's not going to be another war."

Then, striking the wall by the edge of the road
with his stick, he shouted at the top of his
voice:

"*I* won't have another war!"

His mind was as much hag-ridden by sex
as that of John Knox. This preoccupation
made him misjudge the simplest human action.
It even led him round the world in search of a
people that could think genitally instead of
mentally. He had half hoped to find them in the
South Seas, and he was bitterly disappointed
when he found the Polynesians in the same
condition of deliberate sexual allurement as that
in which he had found most Europeans. His
interpretation of human motive was based on a
mixture of hyperæsthesia about himself and
an inability to believe that the most innocent

N

child was not an accomplished hussy. Hence he was always banishing people from his life because they were presumed to have shown malice towards himself or because they had disturbed his austerity by what he believed to be blandishments of manner or attire. So long as Lawrence restricted his self-expression to poems the genius that inflamed him burnt with a dazzling concentrated light; but when in a novel he tried to illuminate with the flame groups of people the effect was too often grotesque. Some of those emanations of Lawrence's own moods incarnate in externally recognizable contemporaries will, if they survive at all, survive only as illustrations of a pathological mental condition.

When one of Lawrence's disciples produces an intelligible code of behaviour from the gospel embedded in the lovely matrix of his work it will be time to contemplate hailing him as a Messiah. So far the interpretation and exposition of Lawrence's message has been most of it pitiable verbiage which, lacking the magic of the master's style, has hindered rather than helped the appreciation of the imperishable qualities in his work. Orpheus met his fate at the hands of infuriated Mænads: Lawrence looks like suffering equally from their kindly intentions. Shelley was spared this competitive dissection by women. Will none of them with-

hold her pen from the ink and tend the memory
of Lawrence in silence?

There is no doubt that the circumstances of
the time helped to unbalance Lawrence. One
could imagine nobody less fitted to withstand
the strain of the Great War under the most
favourable conditions; but for Lawrence,
married to a German wife, pressed for money,
and in poor health, the war annihilated reality.
It plunged him into a miasma of morbid dreams.
And then, as if he were not already suffering
enough, his book *The Rainbow* was seized by
the police in 1915, the futility of which action
was shown when a few years later the novel
was re-issued by another publisher without any
alteration. The effect on Lawrence was disastrous, and the constipated booby of officialdom
responsible for this action deserved a public
purging. What most embittered Lawrence in
this shameful business was the failure of any
prominent author to come to his aid, and it does
cast a reflection upon the state of mind to
which the war had reduced men like Galsworthy
and Bennett that not an effective word was said
on Lawrence's behalf. The whole malodorous
business was carried through with a hole-in-
the-corner pruriency that disgraced English
justice.

Threats of libel actions made unpleasant the
path of one or two other novels, and by then

Lawrence was incapable of perceiving in those threats anything except deliberate persecution. On top of that the volume of poems published in Italy was forbidden ingress to Great Britain, and when finally the police closed an exhibition of his pictures at a London gallery his sense of martyrdom became acute, so that by the time *Lady Chatterley's Lover* was published any sense of proportion left to him had vanished.

*Lady Chatterley's Lover* was unworthy of Lawrence's genius. When the scenes in which certain words never hitherto printed in a serious work of English literature were removed the book became something not unlike a novelette, in which here and there some magical phrase that only Lawrence could have written lights up the tedious unreality of people and place. Was anything of value gained by printing those words expurgated from the public edition of the book? The question of what is and what is not obscene language is obviously unanswerable in any absolute sense; but the belief of some that Lawrence by printing the words he did performed a useful operation on clogged minds is unsupported by any evidence. Contemporary freedom of speech among modern young men and women is not necessarily a sign of healthy frankness; it may be an expression of bad manners:

> Immodest words admit of no defence,
> For want of decency is want of sense.

Thus wrote Lord Roscommon in the middle of the seventeenth century.

When a word has become associated with obscenity through its uses as an expletive, the restoration of it to literature with the full implications of its meaning serves no kind of purpose, and Lawrence's solemn printing of words which, however familiar in speech, are only written by lunatics was either comic or pathetic or both. Unfortunately women, in their recent race to catch up with men in everything, have accepted Lawrence's portentous parade of obscene monosyllables as a direct tip from the masculine stable. They do not apparently realize that it would be an unwarrantable piece of impudence for one man to use such words in the presence of another man unless he were assured of a social, intellectual, and amicable equality that would prevent his freedom of speech from being misinterpreted. Women do not find it difficult nowadays to behave like men, but they often find it extremely difficult to behave like gentlemen. They are apt to lack that particular sensitiveness of the male to the taboo; not unnaturally, since for countless generations of humanity so many taboos were directed against themselves. Probably Lawrence himself was actuated by a desire to break some of these masculine taboos; but the taboos he perceived most readily were the taboos of another class whose difference he resented.

Yet no man was more securely bound by the taboos of his own class. It may or may not be an ethical advantage to destroy all manners, but if manners are to be destroyed, let the destruction be general. To obliterate the relics of feudalism and chivalry and retain the relics of a bourgeois puritanism is unprofitable. Probably Lawrence shocked himself when he wrote the expurgated passages in *Lady Chatterley's Lover*. This emotion would have deceived him into supposing that he was administrating a salutary shock to his readers.

Signs of a poetic revival just before the war were not as easily discernible as the first signs of the novel's progress. Much of the contents of those volumes of Georgian poetry might have been written at any time in the reign of Queen Victoria. There was evidence of facility, but of little else. Most of the verse had the mellow charm of an amber October morning, and the poems of Lawrence among so much that was merely verbal inspiration stung like an icy shower of March.

The war struck authentic fire from several poets who had hitherto written nothing but academic exercises, and it was warming into life fresh poets while it lasted, so many indeed that even after the war the illusion of a poetic revival persisted. Such an anthology of modern life as that made by Sir John Squire is like a pavane of ghosts whose graceful dance is occasionally interrupted by the passage through it of a creature of flesh and blood.

It is not surprising that the experimentalists should have managed so rapidly to assert themselves, and though it is still doubtful at the moment of writing these words whether any of the experimental poets has incontestably proved his claim to be considered a poet at all, and though it is almost certain that posterity will classify imagists and surrealists with the symbolists and other "ists" of the 'nineties, it is absolutely certain that if poetry is to survive as an unmistakable activity of the human mind it can only survive through the success of the innovators. Keats suspected the mortality of old forms more than a century ago, and no poetry written since offers any convincing evidence that he was wrong. Remove the whole body of verse written in Europe since the death of Shelley and in the sum-total of literature the loss would not equal in value what we have lost from the poetry of Greece alone.

It is always a thankless task to name the originator of any movement in the arts, for investigation usually establishes that he merely happened to be the first who caught the public fancy as an exponent of ideas simultaneously prevalent everywhere. Hence, if we fix upon Marinetti and the futurists as the heralds of the peculiar characteristics which at any rate superficially distinguish the literary tendencies of the maturing twentieth century from any literary expression of previous epochs, there will be many to claim the vanguard for other movements like post-impressionism, and as many more to urge that Marinetti's gospel of futurism was too vague to be dignified with so positive a label as movement. Nevertheless, Marinetti threw many old ideas into the melting-pot, and his ta-ra-ra-boom-de-ay method of advertising his creed had a wide effect.

It was appropriate that the revolt against what was felt to be the tyranny of the past should come from Italy, which having served for so many generations as a museum of human effort had gradually acquired the deadening atmosphere of a mausoleum. It would be rash to postulate an absolute law, but the general tendency is for any revolutionary movement in the arts to begin with painting, to pass from painting to poetry, and finally to reach music. During the years immediately preceding the war most of the anticipations of the modern approach to the arts are to be found in painting.

Just before the war broke out there was published a quarterly periodical called *Blast*, a ta-ra-ra-boom-de-ay affair in the Marinetti manner, wherein various young English and American writers and painters affirmed their belief that they were proclaiming or, as I seem to remember they called it, "affirming" the existence of a great European vortex. In spite of the poseurs, charlatans, and hangers-on which any new movement inevitably collects, it was obvious that *Blast* stood for a genuine impulse of fresh creative energy, and nobody who took the trouble to study that publication should have been astonished by a rapid development of the arts after the war along the new lines which it was laying down. So far from precipitating artistic change the war delayed it. What the war did effect was such an unsettlement of the general public as made the task of revolutionary artists a great deal easier than it might otherwise have been. People who had grown accustomed to the upsetting of so many modern mental, spiritual, and physical standards were no longer capable of being shocked as they were capable of being shocked in the peaceful and prosperous 'nineties.

# CHAPTER XXIII

## AFTER THE WAR

AT the end of the war advanced ideas in art and literature seemed to be temporarily concentrated in Chicago, where *The Little Review* was being published. It was in the pages of *The Little Review* that large parts of James Joyce's *Ulysses* first appeared, accompanied in every number by embryonic manifestations of minor creative efforts, in a few of which could be traced as much as the early fœtus of a new form. No doubt many of those who read *Ulysses* as it appeared every month in *The Little Review* except when the police were interfering with publication, supposed at the time that *Ulysses* was only a larger fœtus than any of the others. When in one number of *The Little Review* somebody ventured to assert that *Ulysses* was a major work of literature as significant as the *Divina Commedia* of Dante, the claim seemed preposterous to the point of imbecility; but when in 1922 *Ulysses* was published in full, although many may have decided that the result was a monster, few were prepared to deny that monster a menacing vitality that seemed capable of devouring the whole of contemporary European literature.

Over ten years have passed since *Ulysses* was first published and I find it impossible not to recognize it as the major piece of literature this time has witnessed. That I should be driven into such an admission argues a pessimism about the future of literature which would only be lightened by a positive assurance that the end of the world was, if not actually imminent, by no means as remote as the calculations of astronomers and physicists forecast. I cannot agree with the critics who find in *Ulysses* merely a "powerful confused synthesis of all the mental disturbance, and all the quest for new forms, that stirred in post-war literature." To my mind *Ulysses* is the second part of *Faust* written at last, and the most convincing proof ever penned of the possibility of human damnation, the profoundest revelation of evil ever set down upon paper. Such a revelation could only have been made by an Irishman and a Catholic.

When Lawrence sought to strip the ultimate veil from man in *Lady Chatterley's Lover* the effect was as painfully embarrassing as when an old maid suddenly goes mad and begins to shriek obscenities. That was the result of the provincial Anglo-Saxon revolting against provincial puritanism. It is the shadow of Lucifer which broods over a work like *Ulysses*; the only shadow over *Lady Chatterley's Lover* is cast by a little tin Bethel.

Even much of Aldous Huxley's work is touched by that English provincialism. So long

as he can speak as Aldous Huxley himself a
mocking wisdom flows from his pen. When he
tries to incarnate his ideas in other human beings
the effect is often like that of a don who, having
drunk too much at high table, tries to shock his
academic colleagues afterwards in the Senior
Common Room. Aldous Huxley's influence
over young men both in Great Britain and
America has been considerable, and it is still
considerable. They are awed by his learning
in much the same way as Arnold Bennett remained in awe of it to the end. What they
think are his audacities of thought and expression
give them confidence in their own worldly
knowledge. In the thin soil of youth they flower
and seed precociously under Huxley's watering;
but we have yet to see whether the generation
he has fostered will survive the stress of this
epoch. So far the influence of Aldous Huxley
as a creative writer has been almost entirely
negative, and upon his ability to shed this air
of a perplexed and occasionally exasperated
scholar deprived of academic shelter will depend
his ultimate position.

The rival influence upon the young men
reaching maturity during the second decade
of the century has been T. S. Eliot. His poems,
particularly *The Waste Land*, seemed to offer a
metrical form capable of expressing the new
process of the human mind under the accelera-

tion produced by modern mechanical development. Undoubtedly there was something in the mere rhythm of *The Waste Land* to which young people were capable of giving an emotional response and which made them instinctively acknowledge T. S. Eliot's authority.

*The Waste Land* attempts to compress an epic into four hundred and thirty-three lines, and the poet himself in his elucidatory notes demands of the reader a knowledge of various anthropological works before he can expect to understand what the poem is all about. Provided that a poet can always persuade a certain number of readers to accept him in Sibylline shape, it is difficult for the critic to question his methods or impugn his authority, and hierophancy certainly affords a poet more justification for self-confidence than the contemplation of himself in the battered old rococo mirror that has served so many hundreds of poets. Yet the most sincere hierophant is incapable of protecting his utterances against fraudulent interpretation or simulated understanding, and the danger to T. S. Eliot's renown as a poet may be perceived less in his own vulnerability to criticism than in the discredit into which it may fall through the patent insincerity or incomprehension of his followers. There indeed lies the gravamen of the charge which the old-fashioned critic may bring against all the exponents of what appears to be almost an organic change if not in the process of the human mind, at any rate in the process of mental communication. The most modern literature has produced no criticism of a quality which suggests a permanent change.

It is instinct which tells me that a work like Joyce's *Ulysses* is a major product of creative art; but I have not been fortunate enough to discover any exposition of it which succeeded in weaving it inextricably in with the texture of humanity at this precise moment of man's temporal development. It is true that the æsthetic scheme of the work has been expounded by one or two critics who have been able to avail themselves of the author's personal help; but the technique of a work like *Ulysses* is the least important aspect of it. The mental obfuscation of D. H. Lawrence was lighted even at its darkest by an emotional phosphorescence like that shed by a glow-worm in a midnight lane; but the commentators upon Lawrence have either wallowed in their own sentimental ectoplasm like Middleton Murry or abandoned themselves to uterine ecstasies like his feminine champions.

There is some excuse for the conservative who can only see in the modern manifestations of literature a preoccupation with sex which makes him suspect it as nothing more durable than post-war neurosis. To this preoccupation with sex several causes contribute. First there is the emancipation of women. From the moment that women established themselves as the potential equals of man in opportunity the necessity to uphold the doctrine of romantic love vanished. As early as 1912 it was becoming a habit in America to call any novel in which love predominated a sex novel, and I cannot trace in the nineteenth century any similar application of the word "sex." The disapproval excited by *Jane Eyre* or *The Ordeal of Richard Feverel* or *Jude the Obscure* was not openly charged against the predominance of the sex motive. It was only when women escaped from the conventional epithet of the "fair sex" that the emotions hitherto given a moral significance by terms like love and passion and lust were all merged in sex. It may be observed that even such an adjective as erotic with its exclusively masculine suggestion has almost vanished.

From the days of Eve women have always faced sexual facts with more courage than men. Therefore, as soon as the pretence of having to shelter women from the knowledge which the male had to confront as the inevitable concomitant of experience became superfluous, a freedom of expression both in speech and in writing came into general practice, which particularly in England and America was intensified by the long repression of the nineteenth century. It is noteworthy that in France, where the matriarchal position of women had been more secure than anywhere else in the world, novelists and dramatists had enjoyed what in England was regarded as licence, even if from time to time the state had proceeded against books for offences against public morals. Yet on such occasions there was never any suggestion that the book could do particular harm to women, whereas in England the outraged moralists always protested like seamen that they were thinking of the women and children first.

The most ludicrous interference with an English book of recent years was the suppression of *The Well of Loneliness* by Radclyffe Hall, the theme of which was homosexuality among women. When the editor of a well-known Sunday newspaper had a screaming fit, and by his screams alarmed the Home Office, a prosecution was instituted, the result of which was that thousands of people, who had not been aware that there was such a thing as homosexuality among women and never would have been aware of it but for the advertisement it received at the hands of the Law, were not happy until they had managed to read *The Well of Loneliness* under the impression that they would find out the details of such odd behaviour. It is hardly necessary to add that many novels on the same subject have appeared since without interference and without making the public much wiser about homosexuality among women.

Those who attribute the alleged decay of contemporary morals to the influence of current fiction never seem able to understand that current fiction is always the product of such morals, not the morals of the fiction. A generation which read with avidity a work like *Married Love* by Dr. Marie Stopes was not likely to insist upon the convent-parlour standard of discretion for novelists.

Another contributory cause to the novel's preoccupation with sex was the work of the psychoanalysts which was appearing almost incessantly during the years after the war, until there was not a suburban miss but could twitter about sublimation and repression and her own pet complex. The disproportionate amount of attention to sexual motives in all psycho-analytic speculation and documentation explains the rapid popularity which the Viennese school achieved, and that achievement of popularity has seemed a testimony to their knowledge of human nature. How far they have really helped man to know himself it is as yet too soon to say, but their effect on literature has lain almost exclusively in the direction of falsification, and like every inexact science psycho-analysis has been conspicuously prolific of charlatans.

Perhaps the fundamental reason for the

o

sexual obsession of this period is the problem
of over-population which haunts the back of
every mind. For ages procreation has been the
basis of the sexual act, and now for the first
time in the history of the human race we perceive
the phallus disappearing as a symbol of fertility
and as a consequence a preoccupation with the
moral problem of discovering for it some
symbolic value above that of pleasure. This was
the problem which really tormented Lawrence
more than any other. I once observed to him
that if divorced from its original and natural
intention the sexual act by everybody except
those immediately indulging in it could only
be regarded as a subject for laughter. Where-
upon he fell into a gloom that lasted two days,
at the end of which time he said he believed I
was right. It was shortly after this that he announced his intention of discovering if possible
a race of people who habitually thought not
with their brains but with their organs of generation, whereby he may have hoped to eliminate
that comic side which, as he rightly saw, would
threaten his own work if admitted to be universal.

Once the question of birth control becomes a
topic on their belief in which candidates for
Parliament can be examined by hecklers there
is something a little wild in expecting that the
literature of the time will not reflect such sexual
preoccupation. And it is idle for so distinguished

an upholder of clean reading as Lord Riddell, the proprietor of *The News of The World*, to make speeches entreating novelists to keep sex out of their novels in an epoch when prophylactics against child-birth and venereal disease are openly discussed on the same level of expediency.

The formal abolition of any attempt at procreation can only produce an increasing moral and emotional confusion which must be reflected in literature. However, unless the novel can keep pace with the emotional processes of the mind that the present rate of material development seems likely to bring about, the novel will vanish, because the combination of radio and the cinema already provide for the majority all that is required in the way of mental entertainment, and with the addition of television the competition will become even more severe. The novel can only survive by its ability to offer something which nothing else can offer, and though birth-control may presently be a topic for the Children's Hour at the B.B.C., the moral and emotional confusion of a humanity which has formally rejected its own humanity will for some time yet be a prerogative of the novelist and the poet.

# CHAPTER XXIV

## WOMEN NOVELISTS

NOTHING is more typical of the change in literature during my time than the position which the woman novelist now occupies. It may seem astonishing that a country which produced novelists like Jane Austen, George Eliot, and the Brontës should have continued for so long to regard the idea of women writing novels as something between a joke and an impropriety. Yet it is really only since the war that the lady novelist so dear to the facile pen of the would-be satirical journalist has had to disappear under the numerical and intellectual weight of women novelists. To be sure, we still have our lady novelists, but recent experience as a reviewer leads me to suppose that the species is rapidly approaching extinction, for I seldom come across examples of lady novelists who were not already established as such before the war.

At the moment of writing, when we have excepted Sappho, it can be laid down that the only form of artistic expression in which woman has been able to produce works of art that can be measured by the highest achievement of man is the novel, and it is appropriate that the twentieth century which witnessed the definite emancipation of women should be able to show a body of work by women novelists which no other time has come within measurable distance of approaching. In the year 1933 when I pick up a new author's first novel my average expectation of merit is at least twice as much when I find it has been written by a woman. That many of these young women novelists have lacked staying power is true, but not more true of the young women novelists than of the young men novelists of the present day. That is only one of the characteristics of the swiftly moving times in which we live.

Apart from the women novelists already mentioned in this book, there are few really significant names to add if we limit that list to women writers whose reputation was established or at any rate on the way to being established before the Great War.

May Sinclair was one of the pioneers of the broad path which contemporary women novelists have cut through English fiction. I should not care to attempt to re-read *The Divine Fire* to-day, but when I read it first in 1904 I found it one of the most stimulating and fertilizing experiences of my youth. In her later books Miss Sinclair spoiled her genius by sacrificing it to technique, and though it would be purely romantic to suggest that she deliberately made such a sacrifice to help young women to express what womanhood was peculiarly able to contribute toward the enrichment of the English

novel, I do believe that such an influence was
Miss Sinclair's privilege. Although she has
left behind nothing but a series of failures, her
failures were of greater value to English literature than many of other people's successes. I
remember on one occasion sitting next to her at
a public dinner and hearing her neighbour on
the other side, a former Indian Governor, say to
her in accents from which he was evidently
trying to exclude an ebullient condescension :

"And what do *you* do? Do you write at all?"

"A little," replied Miss Sinclair, in a kind of
faint squeak, the echo of which rebukes me now
when I try without any appearance of condescension to find her niche in the literature of
our time.

Violet Hunt is another stimulating and fertilizing writer who has never received anything
like her due from critics that found in her
breathless, somewhat flurried style insufficient
evidence that she was really writing. Her evocation of the figure of W. H. Hudson at the end of
his days is one of the most masterly pieces of
biographical writing in the English language, and
in some of her novels social historians of the
future will find a truer guide to the state of
society at the end of the nineteenth century and
the very beginning of the twentieth century than
in many works which at the time seemed more
important. She is an utterly feminine writer, and

she has little or nothing in common with the cool-headed young creatures of to-day; but she has a profound sense of life and a wonderful gift of transferring life to the printed page.

There is not much of Violet Hunt's accentuated femininity about Sheila Kaye-Smith. Miss Sheila Kaye-Smith's pages seldom rustle like the silk petticoats of once upon a time. Indeed, she seemed to enter the English novel in rather the same spirit as that in which land girls took up agriculture during the war, and she was one of the first women to assert her right to masculine objectivity without at the same time assuming the name George in order to do so.

The assumption of the name George by women writers—George Eliot, Georges Sand, George Paston, George Egerton, George Preedy occur at once to the mind, and there are several others—offers a nice problem. In spite of the fact that the name has been borne by five British monarchs, George is a name which exposes its owner to a suggestion of good-natured, rather stupid, and completely helpless masculinity. It is noteworthy that Mr. George Bernard Shaw finds it necessary in *Who's Who* to put his George into brackets, and that Mr. H. G. Wells buries his in an initial. Both of them evidently felt early in life that the George in their names would be a handicap. That so many people always refused to take Mr. George Moore seriously may have

been in part due to his Christian name. George
Shakespeare, George Milton, Dr. George Johnson, George Ewart Gladstone. Write their
names thus, and where are they? Yet this was
the favourite name for women who donned the
breeches when they sat down at their desks.
Perhaps the choice of George was dictated by a
suppressed exasperation, as if each woman had
determined to humiliate the male sex by choosing the most typically masculine name and then
rising superior to its implication of masculine
helplessness and good-natured stupidity. At any
rate, I seem to detect in the absence of Georges
among any of the women whose names shine in
literature an expression of security in their
position.

Rosamund Lehmann, Rebecca West, Katherine Mansfield, Storm Jameson, Virginia Woolf,
Victoria Sackville-West, Ethel Mannin, Susan
Ertz, Dorothy Richardson, Clemence Dane, Rose
Macaulay, Mary Webb, Gladys Stern, Margaret
Kennedy, Mary Borden—all these achieved renown in various degrees after the Great War; but
there are no Georges among them, and those of
them who have taken pseudonyms have chosen
feminine ones.

From that list Virginia Woolf stands out, not
merely as the most vitally creative force among
women writers, but as a leader even among men.
If the increasing subtlety and consequent

obscurity of her narrative method may eventually land her where Henry James landed himself, it is difficult to believe that the most perfect English prose any woman has written will not preserve her books against the neglect which has already overtaken those of Henry James. At the same time, an artist must aim at some communication of his intention, and the danger for novelists like Virginia Woolf (and for some of the young poets like W. H. Auden) is that when they lose their contemporary audience the difficulties of comprehension they impose even upon the intelligent and imaginative participators in their own time will become impossibilities for those no longer able to know the external conditions out of which an individual dream was woven. It is possible, of course, to argue that our respect for bygone works of art is merely a conventional piety comparable to the ancestor worship of the Chinese, that whatever was truly valuable in those works of art has already been absorbed into the mind of the human race, and that the apparent long life of bygone masterpieces is due to the relatively lower speed of the human pace and to the relative scarcity of works of art the further we go back to find them. The Greek comic poet Menander, of whose work so little survives, occupies nevertheless as well-assured a position as Aristophanes, not because the fragments we possess of Menander really enable us to judge for ourselves the comparative quality of the two great comic poets, but because we know that Menander's genius was powerful enough to provide the whole substance of the Latin comic drama, and through that of all comic drama since. If Menander had never lived it is impossible to conceive that Molière would have ever lived. It is almost impossible to conceive the existence of Bernard Shaw. Not one person in a hundred thousand is capable even of following the literal sense of Sappho's poetry, let alone of appreciating its inspired song. Yet we could not conceive any development of woman's mind beyond the ability to sustain the idle gossip of the harem without the all too exiguous evidence we possess that over two thousand five hundred years ago Sappho lived and sang. Similarly, a century hence it may be impossible for one writing like myself of the literature in his time to imagine the women writers of his period without the existence of a Virginia Woolf to-day.

Of all those British writers who have been propelled into writing the short story by the impetus of Chekov, Katherine Mansfield came first and remains foremost. For a long while Guy de Maupassant set a European standard for the short story which was less attainable in England than anywhere else. It was only when the eight volumes of Chekov's short stories appeared one by one in translations that young

English writers began to think the short story was easier to write than Maupassant's technique had allowed them to suppose. Volumes of collected short stories are now published every year, the publication of any one of which before 1910 would have seemed a miracle. Yet in spite of the apparent merit these short stories possess they are nearly all affected by the same feeling of mortality as even the best journalism, and I ask myself how it is I am able to recall at least half a dozen of Guy de Maupassant's short stories, at least half a dozen of O. Henry's, and even three or four of Rudyard Kipling's, without being able to recall at the present moment of writing one single short story of Chekov, and of all the short stories written by his English followers only one by Katherine Mansfield. I recognize that this is to carry impressionistic criticism too far. Nevertheless, it does suggest that an inherent weakness of form brought about by the attempt to avoid anything that savours of deliberate machinery may sacrifice more than it gains.

Rosamund Lehmann's first book, *Dusty Answer*, has always seemed to me the best unfolding of girlhood written during this century. It is the only book in which I am tempted to take something like a paternal pride, for the route of *Sinister Street* was fatal to every young man who attempted to march along it himself.

"That was a fearful progeny you begot," said

James Stephens the other day, and ruefully I had to agree with him. In *Dusty Answer*, however, I can feel that a young writer was able to take from *Sinister Street* what was valuable in it and reject unerringly what was not. The result is that I can see in it not an unfortunate parody of my own method of achieving an effect, but a transmutation of my own style through the medium of an original, imaginative, and rich personality into something beautiful which bears no kind of resemblance to *Sinister Street*, but which unless *Sinister Street* had been read in youth might never have been written.

Miss Dorothy Richardson's series of novels about Miriam, which began with *Pointed Roofs* in 1915 and has now reached somewhere round about the ninth volume, has undoubtedly influenced other writers more successfully than they have succeeded in demonstrating themselves to be a comprehensible work of art. They seem to me one of the experiments which had to be made, but the result of which is unsatisfactory. Notwithstanding their experimental form they are essentially novels of surrender to the uneasy drift that is a characteristic of our time. The optimist hopes to discern definite shapes emerging from this drift; but it is often difficult to preserve one's optimism against the critics of a passing epoch who discern in such drift only the evidence of a confusion and a mental darkness likely to become more shapeless and more profound for many years to come. "Trop de beau style pour des prunes," said Taine about the de Goncourts' writing, and cannot that be said with justice about much of our fine-spun stuff to-day?

The novels of Mary Webb never seemed to me to possess much value, and they have always struck me as examples applied to rural England of the same kind of sentimental mysticism as we have seen so much of applied to Ireland and the Gaelic parts of Scotland. The destruction of rural life throughout these islands which has been one of the outstanding results of the last fifty years of mechanical progress has naturally encouraged a romantic or sentimental idealization of the past, and it is perhaps a prejudice created in myself by my knowledge of what a narcotic to action such literature brews that prevents my appreciating it. The music of Delius does not compensate me for the death of folksong. Nor are the Ossianic moans of Fiona Macleod a welcome exchange for depopulated glens.

# CHAPTER XXV

## BEST-SELLERS

VARIOUS attempts have been made to elucidate the mystery of the best-seller. Like the terms "highbrow" and "lowbrow" the best-seller is an Americanism, and it is only since the war that the American influenza of best-selling has been successful in turning popularity into an epidemic. One characteristic of the best-seller of to-day is the briefness of its life. The books of the best-selling novelists of the nineteenth century lasted much longer. Twenty years was by no means an exceptional allowance of time. Many of them lasted half a century. The average expectation of human life is higher to-day; but the life of all the products of human activity is shorter. The present rapid rate of change will probably be accelerated in the future.

The best-seller of to-day in addition to the increased competition of popular books has to face the competition of other forms of ephemeral entertainment like the films and the wireless and daily newspapers. The vogue of a best-seller, after the point of genuine enjoyment has been reached which starts it off, seems to be chiefly due to the urge of curiosity and fashion. It runs through the public like an epidemic, but being apparently dependent on the immediate conditions of the period it affects it leaves the next set of readers immune.

To discover any law in the development of popular taste has always been difficult, but it is impossible to-day, when the potential number of readers is so much vaster than it was a generation ago, that a novelist or a book can become a best-seller without reaching beyond the class of readers to whom it appeals. Charles Garvice, for instance, was a best-seller for many years of this century; but his public was entirely suburban or provincial, and almost exclusively feminine at that.

*The Prisoner of Zenda* in 1894, *Trilby* in 1895, and *The Forest Lovers* in 1898 were popular successes of their respective years. They were three good books, any of which might be read to-day for the first time with pleasure by the average man or woman, none of which if read again to-day by those who enjoyed it when it was published would find its original appeal inexplicable. Round about ten years later *The Garden of Allah* by Robert Hichens in 1905, *The Blue Lagoon* by H. de Vere Stacpoole in 1908, and *The Rosary* by Mrs. Barclay in 1909 were outstanding successes. Few people who pretended to good taste would claim that the second trio was as good as the first ; but no deduction could be made in consequence that a deterioration in public taste had set in with the

twentieth century. What might be argued was
that the increase in the numbers of the reading
public had enlarged the field of potential success.
All six books, to which might be added many
others, were genuine *reading* successes, and the
qualities which attracted interest are obvious.
The epidemic success, when a book was read by
thousands of people without enjoyment merely
because it was a best-seller, was a post-war
feature.

It was in 1921 that the first best-seller of the
American influenza type appeared in this country.
That was *If Winter Comes* by A. S. M. Hutchin-
son, and it should be noted that, although it was
published simultaneously in Great Britain and
America, not until rumours of the fantastic
American success of an English novel crossed the
Atlantic did it begin to sell in Great Britain. I
heard at the time many attempts to explain the
reason why that particular story should have
succeeded in entering almost every home, but I
never heard one which accounted for its overwhelming popularity. It made a sentimental
appeal to the masculine side of human nature.
Mark Sabre was the kind of splendid fellow that
every tired business man could fancy himself in
day dreams. But what was the appeal to women?
And it has always been considered impossible
for a novel to achieve wide success with a solely
masculine appeal. A feature of the *If Winter*

*Comes* epidemic was that half its readers referred to it as *When Winter Comes*.

The next conspicuous success was in 1923 with *The Green Hat* of Michael Arlen. Yet, immensely popular as that was, it did not quite reach the epidemic stage. And it was not a bad book. If it caught the mood of the moment, such a capture was easily intelligible. I think it was in the following year that Miss Margaret Kennedy published *The Constant Nymph*. And that novel did enjoy an epidemic success. I can testify from personal experience that in reading *The Constant Nymph* I was not infected by the germ of American influenza. Naturally prejudiced against best-sellers I avoided reading it when it was first published; but when I did read it a few months later I fell a victim to it like everybody else. *The Green Hat* appealed definitely to women. *The Constant Nymph* appealed chiefly to men over forty and young women. During the epidemic it was read by everybody; but I heard much censoriousness about it from women of taste and experience. The success of *The Green Hat* followed so soon by that of *The Constant Nymph* might seem an indication that public taste was veering in the direction of frankness in the novel. Either of those books published at any date in my time before the war would have raised a puritan howl. Such a theory is disposed of by the next

P

great popular success, *Sorrell and Son* by War-
wick Deeping. This solid book appealing to
solid people might have been written in 1870,
and unlike most best-sellers it has continued to
make an appeal to its public ever since.

In 1927 the translation of Feuchtwanger's *Jew
Süss* ran like an epidemic through Great Britain,
but failed to make a comparable impression
upon America. I shall venture to surmise that
salaciousness may have been the prime reason
for the *Jew Süss* epidemic, a salaciousness
which the most respectable maiden ladies could
enjoy under the disguise of reading a good novel,
and what was even more reassuring an historically
instructive novel. Not that *Jew Süss* did not
possess great merit. Still, we can understand
Arnold Bennett's complaining, when he found
himself saddled with the responsibility of spon-
sorship, that he had never said it was as good as
all that. In 1928 another book enthusiastically
praised by Arnold Bennett struck the popular
fancy. This was *The Bridge of San Luis Rey* by
Thornton Wilder, which may be a perfect
example of the *faux bon*, but which cannot
derive from that possibility an explanation of its
popularity.

It was left for Mr. J. B. Priestley with *The
Good Companions* in 1930 to start the fiercest
epidemic which has yet raged across two continents, and since then no book has enjoyed a

comparable diffusion. Can we argue from the success of *The Good Companions* that the feverish post-war period is at an end? I doubt it. I should prefer to deduce from the success of *The Good Companions* that the great heart of the British public in spite of James Joyce and D. H. Lawrence and Virginia Woolf will always respond with quickened beat to a thoroughly wholesome story, provided such a story can be carried off with sincerity and vitality. That *The Good Companions* would have to be classified under the literature of escape does not seem a reason for condemning it, and our opinion of its value will be dictated solely by our own ideas of what constitutes a refuge.

I have tried to tread cautiously in these comments on best-sellers, because some novelists are strangely sensitive about being described as best-sellers, and in spite of our lip-service to democracy we most of us feel less secure about the value of a popular verdict than we should have felt once upon a time. Comfort may be derived from remembering that *Madame Bovary* was condemned by the critics when it was first published and that its fame was made by the public its author so deeply hated and despised.

# CHAPTER XXVI

## MODERN BIOGRAPHY

IF an examination of best-sellers fails to suggest any perceptible change in the direction of popular taste and even less any perceptible transmutation of the public's mental equipment, modern biographical methods do seem to indicate both. The actual prescription for the present fashion of biography was discovered by Lytton Strachey, and the quacks who have taken advantage of that prescription to make up patent medicines with inferior material should not lead us in the weariness of satiety to underrate the importance of Strachey's contribution to the art of biography. Many circumstances combined to give the Strachey method a vogue. In the first place there was the feline grace of his attack, that ironical neatness which in the case of the reading majority a long rest from Voltaire had made seem so delightfully original. Then there was the charm of the prose which appeared to have been evolved for the very purpose it achieved. On top of the pleasure in these qualities of style there was the pleasure of watching solemn personages undressed like so many naughty children, and on top of that again the reassurance the people of an unsettled and confused post-war world derived from the proof that their predecessors secure in the fastness of the nineteenth century were as vulnerable as themselves to the right kind of weapon.

One danger of the Strachey method of biography is the exposure of the subject to the whims and prejudices of a temperament. If we could imagine the unpublished manuscript of Boswell's *Life of Johnson* coming privately into Strachey's hands and his use of it to write the first life of Johnson, we might doubt if Strachey's biography would provide us with an authentic portrait of Johnson. We should probably miss entirely any knowledge of Johnson's deep piety, which to Strachey would have seemed as much a subject for ironical presentation as the piety of General Gordon or Cardinal Manning. It would be unjust to call Strachey's portraits caricatures, and it would hardly be possible to accuse them even of a lack of perspective. Yet an abuse of chiaroscuro due to excessive virtuosity may produce in effect an equivalent to either. Furthermore, Strachey's chiaroscuro is often deliberately achieved by the artificial lighting of the time and mood in which he was working. There were signs in his last book that this was degenerating into a conventional trick, and certainly none of Strachey's followers has managed to conceal from his readers the method by which he gains his effects.

It may be doubted whether the sum-total of the biographies that have been such a feature of the last ten years has added anything of permanent value either to our knowledge of humanity or to our understanding of history, and if that doubt is found valid it will be because every one of those biographies has interpreted the past in terms of the present. This would not matter if the present were less amorphous than our particular present and if it were not in such a state of ultra-rapid flux as our present happens to be. We cannot judge the value of our contributions to biography until the new development of humanity which, it may be a little rashly, we are inclined to assume has had time to produce biographers of ourselves. It is not worth while to strip the romance from a romantic figure of the past because the particular romance with which that figure was surrounded no longer seems romantic to us. I who knew D. H. Lawrence well can watch already the mythopœic process at work on his personality; but, though I may know it to be mythopœic, I am not therefore in a position to impugn its truth. The ultimate truth of Lawrence as an artist must be the truth that his devotees learn from him, and if he is capable of inspiring a faith, no amount of scepticism on the part of other people will affect it one way or the other. At the same time, it is unreasonable of this period to deromanticize somebody in the past by using the standards of the present unless the present is ready to deny itself the joy of romanticizing its own human products. The future may find that the psychological maze in which we have temporarily lost ourselves was an unnecessary complication of human motive. The more people I know the more I am inclined to believe with Balzac that there are only about a dozen different characters in the human race, and that human conduct is a very much simpler affair than we like to suppose. Material progress has moved forward at such a pace that civilization finds itself bewildered. Bewilderment confuses human behaviour. Hence the appearance of complicacy our behaviour now presents. Far be it from me to plunge headlong into the morass of behaviourism out of the bog of psycho-analysis; but I do believe that there is more firm ground on which one may tread in behaviourism than there is in psycho-analysis. What this age needs above all is a writer like Stendhal. "He lived, he loved, he wrote." Most of our present intelligentsia can only manage to write.

# CHAPTER XXVII

## AMERICAN LITERATURE

ONE of the features of literature since the war has been the rapid advance of the American novel. There have always been plenty of good American novelists; but until the war it would have been true to say that most of the leading American novelists were just a little more conservative than their English confrères. Even as late as 1912 I remember thinking how little American novelists had made of their own country, and how little they seemed to realize how far in a purely material way America was ahead of Europe. Nobody could have derived from Henry James or Edith Wharton the least idea of what America was really like. Indeed most American novelists seemed like transplanted English writers, whose point of view had been slightly modified by its background.

The phenomenon of a great American poet like Walt Whitman, not a line of whose verse could have imaginably been written except by an American, appeared an isolated phenomenon. Owing to being the son of an American mother, familiarity with American literature was constant throughout my youth, and I was never for a moment aware of any profound difference between America and Europe apart from such superficialities as difference of accent. But it was the America of Hawthorne and Washington Irving suitably tempered by Southern prejudice. Books like *Uncle Tom's Cabin* never came my way. Lee of Virginia was the hero, not Abraham Lincoln. Then one day *Leaves of Grass* fell into my hands, and I woke up to the potential influence of American ideas upon the rest of humanity. Some of the fascination that Walt Whitman exercised east of the Atlantic might be compared with the fascination that D. H. Lawrence has exercised west of it. It is not absurd to suggest that Walt Whitman was a happier D. H. Lawrence, the happiness being conferred by the physical vigour fate denied to Lawrence. Moreover, Lawrence was always weighed down by the past, from which obsession of ancient Europe Walt Whitman was free. The war between the North and South had left Walt Whitman triumphant. Ethiopia had saluted the Colours. For Lawrence the European War was a meaningless and useless purgatory of the spirit. Should the American civilization ever succeed in justifying itself as one of the nobler manifestations of human progress, Walt Whitman may present himself to posterity in the light in which English poetry regards Chaucer.

The first American novelist who succeeded in impressing upon Europe the existence of America as something positively and heavily fraught with significance for the rest of the world was Sinclair

Lewis, for it was in his pages that Europe first began to read the origins of the state of mind to which Europe itself was beginning to succumb. In spite of the intervention of the United States in the war, British opinion was the last in Europe to realize how completely the old British domination had been supplanted by an American domination. When Sinclair Lewis's novel *Main Street* was published in England in 1920 The *Times Literary Supplement* dismissed it in half a dozen lines, and it was not until two years later that, with the publication of *Babbitt*, English critical opinion recognized the power of Sinclair Lewis as an expression of the power of the United States. Even to-day English critical opinion is still vaguely bewildered by the award to Sinclair Lewis of the Nobel Prize for Literature. And highbrow opinion is against him in his own country, where the sesquipedalian tramp-tramp of Theodore Dreiser is regarded more reverently.

The last decade has witnessed a remarkable technical advance in American fiction. Writers like Ernest Hemingway, Dos Passos, and William Faulkner have established themselves as influences over Europe. Even in France it is the young American writers who present themselves to the fancy of the Parisian *côterie* as emanations of a vital force in literature, and when we have discounted all the charlatanism and pretence which are inseparably associated with any apparent advance of æsthetic theory we are left with an uncomfortable conviction that the future vitality of the English language will depend more and more on the vitality of the United States. Perhaps the showman instinct of America has created an exaggerated impression of the strength and importance of modern American literary tendencies. A writer like Ezra Pound has been the Barnum of modern literary movements, and performing sparrows like Miss Gertrude Stein have been offered to the public as nightingales.

There is another point of view which only sees in American civilization a synthetic culture produced by an amalgam of various races, every member of which having been uprooted is therefore a potential element of rapid decay. Modern American literature lends support to such a point of view. The technical accomplishment is great, but it does often seem to partake of the kind of technical accomplishment that has gone to the making of American films, those films which at great expense of energy, money and ingenuity leave on the mind an impression that an idiot's tale has been told, full of sound and fury, signifying nothing. And this is the impression that as a reader I derive from some of the most brilliant American novels. While I read, the technical skill of the presentation bewitches my critical faculties into quiescence; but when I look back after a week or two to what I have read, any sense I may have had of creative effort at the time has vanished, and the heart-rending impermanence of it all makes any indulgence in modern American fiction a melancholy enough form of hedonism. Let me hasten to add that impermanence is a characteristic noticeable in the modern fiction of all countries. It is probably an inevitable accompaniment of the external conditions of life. We have not yet faced the fact that novels are read nowadays in the same spirit as newspapers. We have not quite reached the stage of telling the maid to be careful not to throw away yesterday's novel; but it has to be an exceptional novel that leaves as much in the mind as the contents of yesterday's paper.

The existence in America of various clubs and societies for compelling the public to swallow a certain number of chosen books every month has been made necessary by the number of books published annually. Mass production demands mass absorption. The system has been copied in England where the Book Society disentangles every month a few books for its clients. Those who have turned over the pages of the late eighteenth-century and early nineteenth-century novels which are no longer mentioned in compendiums of literature will agree that the average novel of to-day is an incomparably superior affair. Moreover, the standard is rising steadily all the time. When we consider the immense increase in the quantity of books, the world of to-day may be congratulated on its ephemeral entertainment, and it is appropriate that the country which gave the world mass production should have succeeded in raising the standard of the mass-produced novel.

# CHAPTER XXVIII

AN examination of the state of Scottish and Irish literature during the last fifty years reveals a humiliating state of affairs for the Scotsman, and although in the year 1933 there are signs of a new vitality in the Scottish literature of the immediate future, it would be both premature and fond to claim results of more than local interest. No doubt if every writer in English of Scottish extraction were credited to Scotland an imposing list might be drawn up. None would deny to Scotland the honour of claiming Carlyle; but how many would be equally ready to grant Scotland the honour of claiming Ruskin, who by blood was just as much of a Scotsman as Carlyle? Nobody questions the fact that Bernard Shaw in spite of his Scots name is an Irish writer, but comparatively few recognize Norman Douglas as a representative of modern Scottish literature. The fact was that the Kailyard school during the nineteenth century mortgaged Scottish literature to indignity as Sir Harry Lauder and his fellow-comedians have mortgaged Scottish humour. Nevertheless, whatever one may think of the Kailyard school, their representative character cannot be denied. The fiery young Scottish writer of to-day who has revolted from what he thinks a degraded sentimentality is inclined like everybody else to attribute the morals to the fiction instead of the fiction to the morals. A book like *The House with the Green Shutters* by George Douglas would be accepted to-day as a bitter but not greatly exaggerated presentation of small town life in Scotland; but when it was published in 1901 it was regarded as a combination of parricide and matricide in the brutality of its exposure. It was within narrow limitations a good book, but nothing like so good as the repercussions of the shock it caused have made those who have not read it suppose it to be. While the spirit of the nation was oozing away in the pawky sentimentality and Judaic self-depreciation of the Kailyarders, other Scottish writers used cloak-and-sword romance to drug their sense of provincial decline. Of these Robert Louis Stevenson managed to make most of the English-speaking inhabitants of the world dream his own dreams; but Neil Munro and others never succeeded in bewitching any except a few of their own countrymen.

It was not until C. M. Grieve, writing under the name of Hugh MacDiarmid, published *A Drunk Man Looks at the Thistle*, a long poem written in a synthetic Scots dug out from the whole treasure of the Scots language as far back as the Middle Ages, that a new spirit sprang to life in Scottish literature. The nearest approach

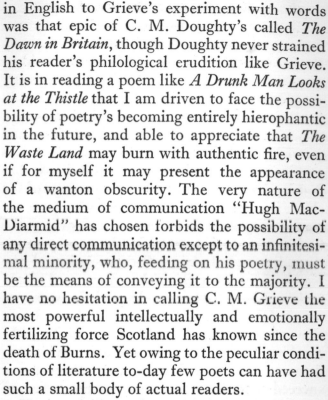

in English to Grieve's experiment with words was that epic of C. M. Doughty's called *The Dawn in Britain*, though Doughty never strained his reader's philological erudition like Grieve. It is in reading a poem like *A Drunk Man Looks at the Thistle* that I am driven to face the possibility of poetry's becoming entirely hierophantic in the future, and able to appreciate that *The Waste Land* may burn with authentic fire, even if for myself it may present the appearance of a wanton obscurity. The very nature of the medium of communication "Hugh Mac-Diarmid" has chosen forbids the possibility of any direct communication except to an infinitesimal minority, who, feeding on his poetry, must be the means of conveying it to the majority. I have no hesitation in calling C. M. Grieve the most powerful intellectually and emotionally fertilizing force Scotland has known since the death of Burns. Yet owing to the peculiar conditions of literature to-day few poets can have had such a small body of actual readers.

Having deliberately avoided mentioning any of the younger generation of English writers I do not propose to single out any of the younger Scottish writers. It is to be hoped that a novelist like Eric Linklater will fulfil all his rich promise, but he will only be handicapped by feeling that he carries big money. Twenty years hence will be time enough to be writing books about the younger generation of to-day.

Ireland was luckier than Scotland in not producing anything like the Kailyard school of writers. Perhaps "lucky" is not the word, for if Ireland had followed the example of the Jews and the Scots by inventing a comic legend about themselves and prostituting their nationality on the stages of music-halls all over the world, they might have demanded the crocodile tears of the Kailyard school to preserve by self-indulgence what they supposed to be their national self-respect. To be sure, there was once a stage Irishman, and his posturings coincided with the "broth of a boy" school of novelists and dramatists. Fortunately political seriousness was proof against the flattery of what was believed to be typical Irish humour.

It is the fashion now in Ireland to deprecate the attribution to writers like W. B. Yeats or J. M. Synge of any specifically Irish characteristics. The political antagonism of a long-oppressed race which at last finds itself with the upper hand cannot forgive the Anglo-Irish or West British ascendancy. Yet an outsider like myself who is in acutest sympathy with the most extreme hopes of the Irish nation may perhaps be able to perceive through the murk of political and religious antagonisms a quality in the Anglo-

Q

Irish writers which had nothing to do with English and which did serve Ireland in a way that her own writers never served Scotland. The Celtic revival lives for ever securely in the pages of George Moore's three volumes of auto-biography *Ave*, *Salve*, and *Vale*, and not even George Moore's exquisite mischievousness can succeed in hiding all the passionate reality that inspired so much absurdity. It is difficult for a Scotsman not to believe that, if Scotland had possessed during the twenty-five years prior to the war a set of North British writers as pro-foundly aware of and as earnestly anxious for the integrity of their country as the West Britons in Ireland were, the condition of Scotland to-day would be far otherwise than it is. We know now that the sacrifice of blood was necessary for Irish freedom; but the West British writers did sacri-fice ink, and that is more than any Scottish writers thought of doing until recently.

After the literary fertility which had preceded the Easter Rising of 1916 it would have been too much to expect that a comparative fertility would mark the next decade or two, whatever the circumstances; but the agony which Ireland suffered for seven years must in any case have wounded literature, and although there are many young Irish writers of outstanding ability, no-body has yet arisen to display what a free and unmutilated Ireland can offer to the machine age. Yet in the work of a young novelist like Francis Stuart we are granted bright glimpses, and it is only a fear of tempting fate that forbids me to cry "*Tu Marcellus eris*."

# CHAPTER XXIX

## AND WHAT NOW?

HARDLY a week before I sat down to begin this book it was my good fortune to meet after an interval of some years James Stephens, the Irish poet. In the course of conversation he commented upon the utter break with the past which humanity is now at the point of making. "Man, as we know him, is finished," he declared. "Plato, Dante, Shakespeare, all the rest of them, no longer mean anything. A new kind of man is beginning to reveal himself. Speed is the basic foundation of this new man. The mind has already begun to change its processes to take advantage of the speed with which every day the body is being more and more richly endowed."

Such was the purport of his speech, though when recorded by me the eloquence seems less convincing than it sounded from his own lips. The personality of James Stephens, which has a fairy quality, touches whatever he says with so beguiling a magic that any listener may be forgiven for supposing that he is being granted a revelation of elfish elemental wisdom. When I listen to the prophets of a new faith, my conservatism is usually undisturbed, because while aware of mental progress I perceive at the same time such evidence of physical regress that the reverence owed to superiority vanishes in a disgust of the imperfect flesh which clothes it. I am haunted by the fancy of a future for man which as it endows him with a mind ever more and more active will curse him simultaneously with the body of a less and less active ape. There are no apprehensions of this kind in talking to James Stephens, which is like being introduced to a new world by Puck himself; and he would be a bold reactionary who despised his prophetic utterance. It seems indeed that, unless some catastrophe of war or pestilence on a scale immensely greater than anything the world has yet known by exacerbating the struggle for existence intervenes to prolong the way of human thought since Genesis, the second millennium of the Christian era will see humanity launched upon a way of thought a thousand times more different from our present ways of thought than ours from the thought of neolithic man.

This is the mood in which I feel inclined to wind up this book. While it seems fairly certain to me that except *Ulysses* no major work of art has yet been produced by those who, aware of the transition from one kind of man to another, are trying to achieve that transition within their own lives, I am perfectly certain that no major work of art will ever be produced again by those who fail to achieve that transition. What could be written or painted or composed by Caucasians of the pre-machine era has been written or painted or composed already, and it seems improbable that other races will not be equally affected by the new kind of existence that the future will rapidly evolve. Such a mood makes it difficult to indulge in the neatness of pigeon-holing with any satisfaction either to myself or the reader.

It is true that in the course of writing this book I have from time to time tried to kick myself as it were out of a nightmare, tried to reassure myself with such phrases as *plus ça change, plus c'est la même chose*, but at the end of the book the nightmare inexorably returns. I cannot believe that the new approaches to literature which are discernible in every country of the world transumed by the material progress of the last quarter of a century are merely a passing phase. We seem to be standing at a point of human evolution when the individual must surrender to the group mind. If Communism can only be fought by the inverted form of it called Fascism, there is no hope for the individual so far as the externals of individuality count. Such a state of affairs must drive the individual who is not content to become a mere ant in one of the great ant-heaps of the future to seek more and more ardently the freedom within his own mind. Already writers are dissatisfied with what they consider worn-out methods of communication. Already some of them have lost the ability to see life at any point in terms of pre-machine man.

The development of women must hasten a collapse of the past, for the mind of woman is so radically different from the mind of man that even were men to succeed in retaining romantic concepts like honour they could not retain them long against the devastating cynicism and directness of women. There will probably be a much wider and a much deeper feminization of men. We may expect to see an intellectual phenomenon like D. H. Lawrence repeated and repeated. It is significant that in all the clumsier forms of herd life the male rules, but that in all highly developed communities such as the bees and the ants the female element rules. No woman, with once again the possible exception of Sappho, has yet written the truth about herself, and in writing it about herself about other women. Those women who have attempted to write the truth have lacked like the Brontës any contact with the life of experience. Charlotte Brontë's angry outburst against Jane Austen may be remembered. She accused her of having no depth of feeling. We may be sure that Jane Austen had as much depth as Charlotte Brontë ; but Jane Austen was not prepared to sacrifice the delicate externality like Mozart's music that became the world and the time in which she wrote. When *Jane Eyre* appeared, women were aghast at the way Charlotte Brontë had betrayed her sex. That book had on the women of her period an effect comparable in violence to the effect which *Ulysses* has had on the men of to-day. Yet while I have met many intellectual men who were genuinely shocked by *Ulysses* I have met few intellectual women who were shocked by it.

It may be argued that this is not the first period in the social history of the world when women have shown themselves ready to take the lead. Queen Elizabeth may be cited. To that I reply that, frank though Elizabeth's conversation was even to the point of brutality, her sexual life was a secret that died with her, and it is by their influence on the sexual life of the future that women will assert themselves. Once they control that they will control whatever art and literature the future may produce. Now it is unimaginable that when women really take charge they will be satisfied with a mode of communication consisting of worn-out masculine symbols. We may see an indication of that in the Sitwells. The really original mind is Miss Edith Sitwell. Without her galvanizing force both her brothers might have seemed no more than posthumous children of the 'nineties. If a Catholic writer is inclined to look forward fearfully sometimes at the literary future, it is because he cannot discern any female Catholic writer of creative force. This is not to underestimate a Willa Cather or a Sheila Kaye-Smith, but merely to point out that there is no Catholic Virginia Woolf. James Joyce, whatever his attitude now toward Catholicism, could not have been produced by any culture except that of Catholicism.

Male Catholic writers are at present necessarily critical of the symptoms of the new world. Most of them preserve a kind of Aristophanic conservatism of attitude. At the same time, though they may laugh at each Euripides as he comes along, most of them in their hearts have to recognize that for good or for ill Euripides must win. Moreover, the Aristophanic attitude of a G. K. Chesterton, which already seems merely old-fashioned to so many, will be entirely incomprehensible to a younger generation whose very fathers were products of a time when the continuity of culture had already been irremediably broken. And we are only at the beginning of it. We must wait until 1950 before we begin to get the serious prose of a generation that was able to listen to wireless in the cradle. If the reading of newspapers began to make language meaningless, what will our language seem to those who have been accustomed to hearing it day in day out in its ever-increasing exhaustion?

I belong sufficiently to this age to apprehend

that the changes in literature we now perceive
are not the fugitive expression of a temporary
condition; but I belong too much to the past to
presume to claim a right of exegesis, and with
these words I shall return to my own dreams of
ways and means to give machine-man as difficult
a course as possible.

# INDEX